SELF-C

SPAIN

The Balearics and the Canary Islands

OTHER SELF-CATERING GUIDES PUBLISHED BY CROOM HELM

Self-catering in Portugal
Carol Wright

Self-catering in Greece, Mainland and Islands
Florica Kyriacopoulos and Tim Salmon

SELF-CATERING IN

SPAIN

The Balearics and the Canary Islands

Making the most of local food and drink

Carole Stewart with Chris Stewart

CROOM HELM
London & Sydney

© 1986 Carole Stewart and Chris Stewart
Croom Helm Publishers Ltd, Provident House, Burrell Row,
Beckenham, Kent BR3 1AT
Croom Helm Australia Pty Ltd, Suite 4, 6th Floor, 64-76 Kippax Street,
Surry Hills, NSW 2010, Australia

British Library Cataloguing in Publication Data

Stewart, Carole
    Self-catering in Spain: making the most of
    local food and drink.
    1. Marketing (Home economics) — Spain —
    Handbooks, manuals, etc.
    I. Title   II. Stewart, Chris
    641.3   TX356

    ISBN 0-7099-4412-8

Typeset in ITC Souvenir Light by
Leaper & Gard Ltd., Bristol, England
Printed and bound in Great Britain by
The Guernsey Press Co. Ltd., Guernsey, Channel Islands.

Contents

1
Introduction

I first visited Spain about 15 years ago, and, although I was enthusiastic about the countryside, the climate and the wonderful beaches, the food left little or no impression on me. Over the years, however, I have made many Spanish friends who have introduced me to authentic Spanish cuisine — cooking for me in their homes and taking me to restaurants and bars where true Spanish dishes are served. To my surprise and delight, I discovered that Spanish food, though not so involved and complicated as French cuisine, has a character all its own, with little resemblance to the bland, uninspired food served up in many tourist resorts in the name of 'international cuisine'.

With this guide, I hope to share some of my discoveries with you and smooth your way to enjoying a holiday with plenty of memorable eating experiences, as well as leaving you with some interesting ideas to adapt and use at home. Unless cooking is a passion, the last thing you will want to do on holiday is to be tied to the kitchen, so I have tried to include recipes that are simple to prepare and will leave you plenty of time to enjoy your leisure.

For you to enjoy eating out to the full, I ask you to go just a little off the beaten track and look for those restaurants frequented by the locals, where the food will be infinitely better and very much cheaper. There is more about eating out in the special section on page 97. Leave behind your misconceptions. Spain, though not a gourmet's paradise, has plenty to offer those who make the effort.

For the diehards, I have included some recipes which will be more familiar to the traveller's palate, and that are more sparing in their use of garlic and oil.

I will help you with your shopping and guide you through the vast amount of produce available throughout the year. I'll

7

explain the different cuts of meat — very strange at first sight — and help you to identify the mind-boggling variety of fish and seafood available. I will give you all the vocabulary you will need for shopping, together with some useful phrases. Try and learn a few for yourselves — any attempt at the language, however hilarious, is appreciated and will be responded to warmly. You will find that Spanish shopkeepers are generally inclined to be more helpful than their counterparts here and will go to a great deal of trouble to find and prepare exactly what you want. The pace of life is slower. Shopping is not so much a chore as a social occasion, so be patient and enjoy the experience.

King Alfonso 'The Wise', a thirteenth-century Spanish monarch, wrote: 'Spain is rich in honeys, abundant with fruits, teeming with cattle, merry with good wine, happy with an abundance of bread and sugar ... well stocked with oil and fragrant with saffron.' The availability of ingredients is an important factor in the development of a national cuisine. The widespread use of olive oil where we would normally use butter is simply because Spain's climate is ideal for the cultivation of olive trees and, broadly speaking, unsuitable for the grazing of cattle. Smaller animals are easier to raise and, as a result, Spanish cuisine has always featured pork, lamb and veal, invariably brought to the table far younger than elsewhere. Chicken is also popular, and there is a wide variety of fish available in the coastal areas.

Garlic plays a prominent role, as well as both hot and sweet green and red peppers, onions and tomatoes. Almonds, extensively cultivated throughout Spain, are often ground and used as a thickening agent for soups and stews, imparting a very distinctive flavour.

There is an enormous variety of fruit and vegetables with the warm seasons coming early and lasting for a long time. A visit to the local market just to look at the riot of colour and the massive selection will prove a delight.

The high quality of local ingredients has been a major influence on the way in which Spanish food is prepared. If the fish is fresh from the sea, why smother its delicate flavour in a heavy sauce? Why treat tender young cuts of veal, lamb or pork in any other way than simply roasting, grilling or frying? This is not to deny that there are many excellent sauces, soups and casseroles. It is just that good Spanish cooking concentrates primarily on the freshness and quality of the ingredients rather than attempting to mask their natural and sometimes delicate flavours.

The sixteenth and seventeenth centuries were the golden age of Spain, when its empire extended to most of Europe and more than half the New World. It was during this period that outside influences began to contribute to the development of a distinctive, though regionally diverse, national cuisine. Spanish chefs were much in demand by the crowned heads of Europe and many of today's classic recipes derive from their work. In 1637 the chef to Philip II of Spain noted down his recipe for *tortilla de la caraga* — the forerunner of the famous French omelette. The Spanish Infanta's chef first prepared the puff-pastry commonly known as *feuillette*, while, in the Spanish town of Mahón, the capital of Menorca, that most classic of all French sauces — mayonnaise — was devised and adapted from the ubiquitous Spanish sauce: *ali-oli*.

Spain has a stormy history of war and occupation by foreign powers. Celts, Romans, French and Moors have all, at one time, held sway over the Iberian peninsula, and each has left an indelible stamp on the development of Spanish cuisine. There is little evidence pointing to any outstanding gastronomic achievements in early Celtic cultures, but there is certainly something of these age-old influences in the cuisine of the Basque and the Catalan areas. It was the Romans who gave to Spain two of the most important elements of its culinary tradition — oil and garlic — and, although there was already a flourishing viticulture, the Romans promoted and refined the techniques and left behind them a wealth of expertise in the production of fine wines, which is still much in evidence today.

The Moorish occupation of the Iberian peninsula lasted for over 700 years, bringing with it new methods of cooking and imparting a distinctly Middle Eastern flavour to much of Spanish cuisine, particularly in the south. During this period Spanish wine production went into decline, with many vineyards uprooted as a result of the Koranic prohibition of alcohol, but the Moors enriched the culinary repertoire in other ways by introducing sugar-cane, black pepper, cumin, nutmeg and almonds. Saffron was also a new spice which took well to Spanish soil. Today it features widely in Spanish cooking, in particular in the classic Spanish dish, *paella Valenciana*.

The Moors planted the first citrus trees in Spain, although the sweeter, eating oranges were brought to Spain from China by the Portuguese. Both kinds of citrus thrived in Spanish soil. The Moors also left the Spanish with a well-developed sweet tooth, evidenced by the popularity of specialist cake-shops still found in all parts of Spain.

The discovery of the New World greatly enhanced an already flourishing Spanish cuisine. Such basic ingredients as potatoes, tomatoes and maize were all brought back from the Americas by the Spanish and introduced into Europe, together with green and red peppers and cocoa.

REGIONAL COOKING

Spain was once divided into a number of small kingdoms and principalities, each fiercely defending its own customs, traditions and individuality. Geographically speaking, the peninsula is naturally divided by steep mountain ranges (Spain is the second most mountainous country in Europe), deep gorges and ravines and vast expanses of dry scrubland. The difficulty of travelling from region to region contributed to the somewhat isolated development of regional cooking traditions, while climatic variations affected the types of produce suitable for cultivation. It is said that 'in the north they stew, in the centre they roast and in the south they fry', and this indeed gives a rough idea of the basic differences between the cooking of the different regions.

With the improved communications of the twentieth century, there has been a gradual merging of ideas, and many of the classic Spanish dishes — *paella*, Spanish omelette, chicken with garlic sauce — are available through-out the country.

Catalonia (Costa Brava and Costa Dorada)

Catalonia enjoys one of the most privileged positions, geographically speaking, in Spain. An extensive coastline, wild mountain ranges and lush pasturelands have given to Catalan cuisine an abundance of produce, meat, game and fish. Catalonia's borders once encompassed a substantial part of southern France, and this has contributed to its becoming one of the most gastronomically inventive regions of Spain. It is noted for its superb sauces — in particular *romescu*, a delicious fish sauce, red in colour and made from tiny red peppers and ground almonds. The sauce can be very fiery and should be approached with caution.

Hearty soups filled with beans, pasta and sausages — a Catalan speciality — are delicious and wholesome, often served with thick slices of meat-loaf. Wild mushrooms, available at the beginning of autumn, are often cooked with garlic and parsley and served as an accompaniment to sausage or eaten on their own. Try casseroled chicken with aubergine and tomatoes, flavoured with aromatic herbs, or *zarzuela*, a magnificent concoction of white fish and seafoods swimming in a spicy tomato sauce.

Catalan salads are wonderful. *Esqueixada*, a mixture of cod, beans, pickled onions and tomato, is well worth looking out for. For a more piquant taste, *xato de Sitges* mixes together anchovies and tuna fish in a sauce of olive oil, garlic, red pepper and ground almonds.

Sausages are very popular throughout Spain and the islands, and Catalonia offers an enormous range. *Butifarra de Cataluna* is a rich pork sausage, flavoured with garlic, cinnamon and cloves. It is often used as a filler for *tortilla Ampurdanesa*.

A speciality of Catalan cuisine is the combination of fruits with meat and poultry and *oca con peras*, baby goose with pears, is an unusual and delicious example.

Caracoles, snails, are popular in Catalonia and are usually served with hunks of crusty bread and a sizzling hot garlic sauce.

Valencia (Costa Blanca)

Rice has been grown in this region since Moorish times. The landscape is lush and comparatively flat on the coast, quickly rising to a rugged mountain interior. The plain of Valencia supports orange, olive and almond crops, while the long coastline yields seafood in plenty. The most famous dish is *paella*, named after the shallow, heavy pan in which it is cooked. A *paella*, which ideally should be cooked over a wood fire in the open air, will always contain rice, flavoured and coloured with saffron, and a variety of vegetables in season — peas, peppers, onions. *Paella Valenciana* adds crisply fried pork or chicken, while *paella Alicantina* contains, in addition, a selection of seafood such as prawns, mussels, crab, white fish and octopus. *Paella* is delicious and filling but sadly it is often badly prepared both in Spain and abroad. However, it is worth searching for a good *paella*, and if you are kept waiting while it is being prepared, don't be impatient: this will be a sign that the *paella* is being freshly made, and the chances are it will be excellent.

In Valencia, too, try the local spicy stews with rabbit, chicken and pork, or hunt for a restaurant which serves roast suckling pig — an expensive dish but worth every penny. There is an enormous variety of seafood — prawns, lobster, swordfish, sole, mussels and squid. The squid is often sold from stalls and bars deep-fried in batter. It is quite delicious and looks a little like fried onion rings.

An unusual speciality of the region is whole fish, packed in rock salt, baked and brought to the table still encased in the salt jacket. The salt preserves the flavour of the fish but does not, as you might expect, impart an unduly salty flavour to the flesh. Great use is made of piquant sauces, particularly with deep-fried shellfish, the most famous being a creamy sauce of garlic and olive oil known as *ali-oli*.

Andalucia (Costa del Sol)

Andalucia is the largest region in Spain. It is a dry, arid province best suited to the cultivation of olive and orange trees. The hotter climate of this region has strongly influenced the cuisine, and the heartier dishes of Catalonia and Valencia are less common here. Generally speaking cooking methods are based on the frying-pan and the skill of the Andalucian chef with this utensil has reached almost virtuoso proportions. It is here that mounds of tiny fish are fried very lightly, but to crisp, sizzling perfection in just a little fragrant oil.

Gazpacho, now widely available all over Spain, is an Andalucian creation. It is essentially a chilled 'salad soup' and, although there are numerous variations, the basic ingredients are onions, tomatoes, peppers, cucumbers, bread, olive oil and garlic. *Gazpacho* is sometimes served in a mug and sometimes in a bowl accompanied by a variety of garnishes — crisp fried croûtons, diced cucumber and chopped onions or peppers — making a wonderful contrast to the cold smoothness of the soup.

Asparagus is a popular vegetable in Andalucia and the wild variety is an essential ingredient in many Andalucian dishes, either as a base ingredient or as a lavish garnish.

Chicken, veal and game are well liked and are often prepared with wine or sherry sauces, but it is fish — often a 'cocktail' of several different varieties — that features most widely on the Andalucian table.

Spanish omelettes are popular here and eggs are used in another popular regional dish, *huevos a la Flamenca* — a mouth-watering mixture of ham, peas, asparagus, tomatoes, *chorizo* sausage, potatoes and eggs.

The Balearic Islands — Mallorca, Menorca, Ibiza and Formentera

The style of cookery in these islands, particularly Mallorquín cuisine, bears some similarity to that of Catalonia. There are, nonetheless, a wide variety of local dishes and quite a few of the dishes served throughout Spain originated from one or other of these islands.

Mallorca's mountains provide the perfect habitat for many species of game while its mild climate and rich soil supports a great variety of fruit and vegetables. The island is dotted with olive trees and literally millions of almond trees. The blossom is quite exquisite when in flower.

Sobresada is a typical Mallorcan sausage. It contains pork, pork tripe, salt and cayenne pepper and is, unusually for a Spanish sausage, soft and smooth in texture and suitable for spreading on bread.

Roast suckling pig goes down well here, as does *sopa Mallorquina* a delicious hearty soup so full of vegetable ingredients that you can almost stand your spoon up in it.

Menorca is comparatively flat and windy, but lush farm-land in the north provides rich grazing to support the island's flourishing cheese industry. *Queso de Mahón*, a dense, yellowish white cheese dotted with tiny pinprick holes, is popular everywhere in Spain. It was here in Mahón, the capital of the island, that *mahonesa* (mayonnaise) was first invented.

Quail is one of the specialities of the island, although over-hunting has severely depleted numbers and it is not so commonly available today.

Ibiza and Formentera are more redolent of southern Spain in character, with regard both to architecture and to their cuisine. Here the Moorish influence on the cooking tradition is strongly felt and the Andalucian flair with fried fish is every-where apparent.

The Canaries

In spite of their geographical distance from Spain, these islands still have an unmistakably Spanish atmosphere, and many of the dishes common on the mainland are popular here. The main difference lies in the sub-tropical climate, which allows for the cultivation of certain crops that are not available on the mainland, including sweet potatoes, avocado pears, tiny sweet tomatoes, early potatoes, mangoes, tiny Canary bananas and papayas.

Visiting the Canaries you are likely to come across a substance called *gofio*. There is no direct translation of this word. Basically it is grain — either maize, barley or wheat — which is toasted and then ground to a fine powder. The islanders add *gofio* to soups, stews, milk, biscuits and cakes as well as mixing it with water to make a thick paste and eating it as an accompaniment to some foods in the same way as bread is eaten in other parts of Spain.

Wherever you go in Spain you will find a wide variety of dishes on offer, and the excellence of the markets will enable you, with the help of this book, to create almost any of the recipes mentioned, however far away you may be from the region of origin.

SPANISH EATING HABITS

If you attempt to emulate Spanish eating habits you will begin to realise that there is another reason for that great Spanish tradition — the siesta. Lunch (*el almuerzo*) is a very important meal to a Spaniard and will invariably consist of three courses and a substantial quantity of wine to wash it all down. Dinner (*la cena*), usually eaten later than here, is another three-course affair accompanied always by wine and usually followed by coffee and cognac. In between these two daily feasts (and besides eating a light breakfast), the Spanish will often snack on savouries or indulge their taste for pastries at 'elevenses' or teatime. Don't imagine that the portions are small: a true Spaniard would disdain the tiny portions served in our fancier continental-style restaurants.

Eating out is a way of life in Spain, and the Spanish eat and snack out often. The wonderful climate encourages leisurely evenings in open-air cafes, bars and restaurants, and the prices (except in the more exclusive restaurants in the tourist areas or major towns) are much more reasonable.

Tapas

Tapas, one of Spain's greatest eating traditions, originated in Andalucia, although a wide variety of *tapas* can be found all over the mainland and in the islands. A *tapa* is basically a bite-sized morsel of food. *Tapa* means 'lid', and, traditionally, drinks were served with a tiny plate over the top of the glass carrying a few plump, juicy Spanish olives or a slice of prized *serrano* ham (a wind-dried ham somewhat similar to *prosciutto* but coarser and stronger in flavour).

Some *tapas* bars display lists of the selection available that day on blackboards, and in other establishments the *tapas* are laid out on or under the counter. Often these places offer *raciones* — the same as *tapas* but simply more generous portions. For garlic lovers, try portions of sizzling garlic mushrooms and prawns or tiny fried fish and deep fried meatballs. An unusual *tapa*, and not to everyone's taste, is *pajaritos* — tiny birds deep-fried and eaten whole, head, beak, bones and all. Understandably, this particular delicacy is not so widely available nowadays.

For those who are happy not to sit down to a heavy meal at night, especially after the rigours of a three-course Spanish lunch, the evening can be well spent *tapas* bar-hopping, washing down a different *tapa* at each stop, with a delicious glass of sherry or *vino tinto*, red wine. But be careful, you'll drink more than you realise. *Tapas* are available throughout the day, and one or two make a light and satisfying lunch. Go with a group of friends and order the whole range. Or even better, make your own, and serve them instead of lunch, with your evening drinks or as an appetiser to dinner.

2
HOW TO USE THIS BOOK

Phrase-books can be infuriating. Often they will tell you how to ask for something on one page, but list the items you are actually asking for on another. Although this is not a phrase book, I have included phrases and vocabulary after most of the chapters. There is some repetition, but I think you will find the system more practical.

If you have decided to prepare certain recipes from the book, make your shopping list and then refer to the appropriate chapter to check for hints and tips on buying that particular ingredient. The fruit and vegetable, meat, poultry, game and meat products and fish and seafood sections, contain comprehensive listings and descriptions of everything you are likely to want to buy. For certain foods, such as lobster, prawns, artichokes and asparagus, I have included basic preparation methods in the appropriate sections. Further recipes for most of them are included in the recipe chapter.

The herbs and spices, sundries and staples chapter is more of a hotch-potch. It would be impossible to list every type of foodstuff available, but you should find reference (or vocabulary) here for all your basic needs.

I have given an indication of fruit and vegetable seasons, but Spain is a big country and climatic variations — alpine to sub-tropical — make it impossible to be precise. You will be able to tell if the produce is in prime condition by referring to the guidelines in the appropriate sections.

3
LOCAL FRUIT AND VEGETABLES

FRUIT

There are few fruits that are not available somewhere in Spain and the islands, although the more exotic varieties are imported and therefore more expensive. The quality of the fruit is generally very high, and it is usually far cheaper than it is here. Take, for example, strawberries: they are generally available from April onwards in most parts of Spain and can cost as little as 100 pesetas for 2 kilos.

In hot weather, when puddings are too heavy a finish to most meals, fresh fruit is an excellent and healthy substitute. I have included recipes for desserts, but I strongly suggest that you follow the Spanish lead and finish your meal with cheese or fruit. In the cheaper restaurants, it's all you are likely to get anyway, save the omnipresent *flan*.

Fruit-sellers are usually quite happy for you to select your own fruit, and with the enormous selection available, you will find shopping for fruit a pleasure.

Apples (*Manzanas*): all year

You will recognise many of the varieties of apples and there is generally a good selection available throughout the year. The best Spanish apples are grown in the northern regions of the peninsula where the colder climate is more suited to their cultivation.

Apricots (*Albaricoques*): May-December

A popular fruit and quite reasonably priced. Choose unblemished samples without any green tinge.

Apricots

19

Avocado Pears (*Aguacates*): all year

The two varieties of avocado available in Spain are the smooth, green-skinned type and the black, rough-skinned type known as 'alligator pears'. Both these types are delicately flavoured, and should be eaten when the pale green flesh has ripened to the consistency of soft butter. They can be used in salads, sauces and soups and, surprisingly, as a flavouring for ice-cream but avocado is most frequently eaten on its own with a simple dressing. The avocado should be cut lengthways, with a sharp knife, around the central stone. The stone should be discarded and the avocado can then be eaten in its skin with a spoon. It is excellent with an oil and vinegar dressing or stuffed with prawns in a light mayonnaise.

Bananas (*Plátanos*): all year

Platano usually refers to the little Canary island bananas, sweet and tasty, while *banana* will get you a bigger fruit, probably imported from South America. The tiny Canary Islands bananas are especially delicious and you should try them at least once. Bananas with a tinge of green will ripen very quickly and it is often better to buy them like this, especially when you plan to keep them for a few days before eating.

Blackberries (*Zarzamoras*): April-June

Usually sold in small tubs. Toss the fruit around before you buy to ensure that the bottom layer is as good as the top, and that there is no mould. Check the bottom of the tub. If it is stained this will indicate that the fruit is either over-ripe or crushed.

Blackcurrants (*Grosellas Negras*): April-June

Usually sold in small tubs. Selection as for blackberries.

Cherries (*Guindas or Cerezas*): May-June

Spanish cherries are quite delicious. There are three main varieties. The dark red *bigarreau* — large and heart-shaped with a good, strong flavour. The Emperor Francis, also dark red in colour, and, later in the season, the almost black variety. Reject fruit which is scarred and brownish at the point where the stalk meets the fruit.

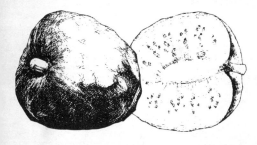

Custard apples

Custard Apple (*Chirimoya*): May-February

An unusual fruit, rarely seen here. The custard apple is about the size of a large apple with a green, 'quilted' skin, and looks rather like a hand-grenade. The flesh is sweet and full of little black seeds which should be discarded as you eat. Cut the fruit in half and eat with a spoon. When you buy this fruit it should be soft to the touch, with no brown scars.

Figs (*Higos*): June-September

The two main types of this delicious fruit are round-shaped and a long, almost pear-shaped variety. The skins are dark purple or green in colour. This fruit becomes much cheaper later in the season. Choose plump fruit with firm, unbroken skins. A sour smell indicates over-ripe fruit.

Grapefruit (*Pomelo*): all year

You can buy both the yellow-fleshed and

the pink-fleshed varieties. Look for fruit with a smooth, fine-textured skin. A coarse skin often indicates that the fruit will not be as juicy as it should be.

Grapes (Uvas): **May-Dec**

Grapes are usually excellent and cheap. Don't reject green grapes that have a slightly pinkish tinge. This does not mean that they are not ripe and, in fact, they will usually be sweeter.

Lemons (*Limones*): **January-June**

Lemons are at their cheapest and best from January to June but they are, of course, available year-round. Don't choose lemons with coarse-grained skin or with an over-swollen point at the end, as the fruit will not be juicy.

Limes (*Limas*): **March-November**

Limes are an excellent alternative to lemons, particularly in gin and tonic. They are generally much cheaper in Spain. Choose fruit that has a good, even, green colour.

Mangoes (*Mangos*): **May-December**

King of the tropical fruits, mangoes are a delicious, sweet, fragrant fruit. Although they are not exactly cheap in Spain, they are generally better value than here. The fruit varies in size and shape — from heart-shaped to kidney-shaped, or long and oval — with colours ranging from golden to rosy-red, peach and green. The fruit should be cut in half around the large central stone and pulled apart. The juicy flesh can be eaten with a spoon. Select samples with good, unblemished, smooth skin, which are soft to the touch. A slightly under-ripe mango will soften quickly if left in the sun. You will need plenty of napkins — it is impossible to eat this delicious fruit without getting covered in sticky juice.

Melon

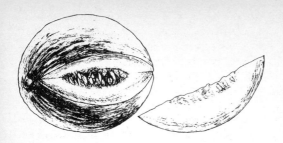

Melon (*Melón*): March-December

Five main varieties are available, all of which you are likely to recognise. Charentais, a smaller-sized melon, has a green/yellow skin with faint longitudinal indentations. The Cantaloupe is similar but squatter in shape, with a slightly roughened skin. Its flesh is heavily scented, and it should be covered if kept in the refrigerator as its perfume will permeate other foods. The Honeydew has green-yellow wrinkled skin with light green stripes. Finally, the water-melon, with its dark green skin and pink, juicy flesh. All melons should be eaten ripe. Press the fruit gently at the blossom end. It will yield to slight pressure if it is ripe. Unripe fruit, left in the sun, will be ready to eat very soon.

Oranges

Oranges (*Naranjas*): all year

A number of varieties are available. The oranges you will see growing in streets and squares, particularly in southern Spain, are the Seville variety (*naranjas amargas*), used for the making of marmalade. They are very bitter and should not be used for eating. The navels commonly available in Britain are ideal eating oranges. For orange juice, look for the *furtes* type, distinguishable by their thin skins. You may come across the *ortanique* — a cross between an orange and a tangerine. The skin is thin, relatively easy to peel, with an orange/yellow colour and very juicy flesh. Satsumas, available

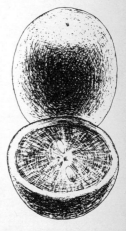

widely in Britain, can also be purchased here. With all the orange varieties, look for samples with fine-grained skins and reject any that are puffy or coarse-grained.

Peaches (*Melocotones*): May-September

Usually of excellent quality. The fruit should yield slightly to pressure and should have a good overall colour with no tinges of green.

Pears (*Peras*): May-December

It is quite easy to choose an over-ripe pear. Unless you wish to eat the fruit immediately, it is better to purchase rather firm samples. Pears ripen from the inside outwards, so a soft exterior can mean an over-ripe centre. You will recognise the Comice variety but the Agua type is worth trying. It is a small pear that stays green and should be eaten crisp. The flavour is lovely.

Persimmons (*Nísperos*): September-February

The persimmon resembles a tomato in appearance and ranges through yellow and orange to red in colour. Under-ripe persimmons are very astringent, but, as they ripen, they develop a delicious, sweet flavour with only a hint of sharpness. Select fruits with a glossy skin and with the stalk firmly attached. To eat, wash thoroughly and remove the stem. The pulp can be eaten with a little added sugar to taste, or pureed and used for ice-cream, jams and a variety of puddings.

Pineapple (*Piña*): all year

Choose pineapples that are heavy for their size and firm to the touch with a definite, sweet perfume.

Plums (*Ciruelas*): May-September

The darker-coloured varieties are most common in Spain and range from a rich, deep red to almost black. Choose unblemished, bright-skinned fruit that yields to slight pressure.

Pomegranates (*Granadas*): June-February

The pomegranate is a hard-skinned, rounded fruit with a colour ranging from whitish pink to deep red. It can be the size of an orange or as large as a grapefruit. When you cut open a pomegranate you will find that the translucent pink flesh is divided into 'cells', each containing a seed. Eat the flesh with a spoon, discarding the seeds as you eat. The flesh has a refreshing, slightly astringent flavour.

Raspberries (*Frambuesas*): April-September

Sold in small tubs. Check that the bottom layer of fruit is as good as the top.

Redcurrants (*Grosellas Rojas*): April-July

As for raspberries.

Tangerines (*Mandarinas*): all year

Good value and usually of a very high quality and with the advantage that they are much easier to eat than oranges.

VEGETABLES

It is possible to buy almost any type of vegetable in Spain, whether indigenous to the country or not, although rare, imported varieties are often quite expensive. Spain's climate allows for the growing of a wide range of vegetables, and in this section I have listed all the major types available, together with brief descriptions, and guidance where necessary on how to select the pick of the crop, and basic preparation methods.

Vegetables play an important part in the Spanish diet. They are frequently served on their own but they are also widely used as ingredients for soups and stews and, particularly in southern Spain where traditional cooking methods have had to develop without too much reliance on fresh water, vegetables are often sautéed or lightly fried.

Given the wide range of geographical and climatic conditions found in the Iberian peninsula and the islands — from the sub-tropical Canaries to the Alpine slopes of the Pyrenees or Sierra Nevada, and the arid, almost desert regions of the centre and the south — there are few types of vegetables that are not cultivated somewhere in Spain. But it pays wherever possible to buy vegetables that are in season locally. As with fruit, seasons as we know them, start much earlier and last much longer in Spain, and certain vegetables that we are used to seeing only for a short time in our markets will be on display in prime condition for much longer in Spain. Certain staples such as onions and potatoes, are available throughout the year.

If you select your vegetables carefully, the quality will generally be high, and you will find that the prices are cheap. It is only the root-crops, such as turnips, beetroots and swedes, which often do not measure up to our standards, although generally, potatoes are good. But who wants to eat turnip and swedes while basking on the shores of the Mediterranean?

Shop-keepers will often allow you to select your own vegetables and this is quite important if you wish to choose vegetables that are uniform in size and quality. Spanish vegetables are seldom graded and frequently large, small and medium samples, of varying degrees of quality and freshness, are all lumped together in the same sack.

Frozen vegetables are easily obtainable in supermarkets and hypermarkets and the quality is easily as good as their equivalents elsewhere. They are, of course, never such good value for money as fresh vegetables.

Artichokes (*Alcachofas*): October to May

Spanish artichokes are at their cheapest and best from November through to January. They are usually smaller than other European varieties and are cultivated all over Spain and the islands. The artichoke resembles a rather plump thistle, and, although the flesh in the base of the leaves is edible, it is the heart of this vegetable with its delicate flavour that is most prized. When you are selecting your artichokes, look for specimens that are uniformly green, with leaves that are tightly packed around the base. The outer leaves should be supple, so refuse any with hard tips, as this is a sure sign of old age.

Artichokes are not eaten raw. To eat a cooked artichoke, pull off a leaf with your fingers, dip the base of the leaf into melted butter or sauce and then scrape off the soft flesh between your teeth. When all the leaves have been removed the heart is exposed. Remove and discard the fine hairs surrounding it and eat with a knife and fork. It is a good idea to provide finger-bowls when serving artichokes as an appetiser.

Artichokes are eaten simply boiled, with the addition of a butter sauce, or served cold with a vinaigrette or hollandaise sauce. They can also be fried, baked with a stuffing, used to make soups or incorporated into salads. Often, the hearts are served on their own and it is possible to buy artichoke hearts in tins.

Basic Preparation

Cut off the stem of the artichoke with a sharp knife and pull off any damaged or scarred outer leaves. Trim off the points of the remaining leaves and then turn the artichoke on its side and slice off the top third. Rub the vegetable on the cut parts with lemon. Spread the leaves apart and pull out all the prickly leaves surrounding the heart. With a spoon, scrape away the hairs and then squeeze lemon juice into the centre. Press the artichoke back into shape. Cook in a large saucepan (not aluminium or iron as this will discolour the flesh, giving it an unappetising grey colour) filled with boiling water for 15-20 minutes or until the base is tender when pierced with the point of a sharp knife. Remove the artichokes and drain. Serve with a sauce.

Artichoke

27

Asparagus (*Espárrago*): March-June

Asparagus is a member of the lily family and was highly prized as a vegetable by the Romans. It has a unique and delicate flavour. It is cultivated throughout Spain and also grows wild, particularly in the Mediterranean coastal regions. You will often see children selling bundles of asparagus at the roadside or in restaurants and cafes.

The wild variety is sometimes available earlier than March but whichever type you choose, asparagus is well worth buying, as it is quite delicious and considerably cheaper than here. Eat it on its own as an appetiser or in omelettes, soups and as a garnish for poultry and fish dishes.

Cultivated asparagus can be pencil-thin or as thick as your thumb. It can be white, often with a purplish tinge, or green. The white variety is usually more expensive and has a very delicate flavour. The cultivated green variety has a more marked flavour, and the wild variety, much more spindly than its cultivated cousins, has an even stronger taste. Choose asparagus that has fresh, unwrinkled skin with closed, compact tips. Avoid any samples that have tall, flat stalks and broad, woody bases. Allow about six spears per person with the larger, thicker variety and about twice that amount for the wild variety.

To keep asparagus as fresh as possible, cut off the ends at the point where the spears become less tender and supple and stand them, tips upwards, in a jar filled with a few inches of water.

Basic Preparation

Peel or scrape the stalks with a sharp knife, thickly at the butt end and very thinly towards the tip. Scraping is only necessary with the larger, cultivated variety. Wash the stalks and tie the asparagus together in bundles. Place the bundles, butt ends downwards, in a saucepan of boiling water and simmer rapidly for about 15-20 minutes, or until the stalks are tender when pierced with the point of a sharp knife. If a suitable saucepan is not available, put the asparagus in a shallow baking dish, half filled with boiling water, and, keeping the tips clear of the water for the first 10 minutes of cooking, simmer until tender. This is important as the tips cook much more quickly than the stems, and will disintegrate before the rest of the asparagus is cooked. Serve hot, or cold, with a melted butter sauce.

Aubergine/Eggplant (*Berenjena*): January to October

The aubergine is a member of the potato family and is one of the most popular vegetables in the world. The two varieties most commonly grown in Spain are either dark purple in colour or purple and white. Select samples which are shiny, uniformly coloured, firm and heavy in relation to their size. Don't buy aubergines that are wrinkled or have scars, cuts or any indentations in their skin. Aubergines can be cooked while in their skins, sliced and fried, baked with a stuffing or stewed. If you are frying your aubergines, slice them first, sprinkle with salt and leave to drain for at least half an hour. This removes excess moisture and makes them easier to fry.

Aubergines

Beetroot (*Remolachas*): all year

Generally speaking beetroots are not of such high quality as those grown in England. In Spain they are mainly used as a relish and sometimes added to salads. Choose small samples with unbroken skin. Avoid misshapen or scarred beets or those with long whiskers. It is rare to find them pre-cooked.

Basic Preparation

Trim foliage to within one inch at either end. Wash well, but be careful not to damage the skin or the beet will bleed and lose its colour during cooking. Put the beets into a large saucepan of boiling water and simmer until tender. This will take between one and four hours depending on size. The vegetable is cooked when the skin rubs off easily. Don't pierce the beetroot with a knife as this will cause it to bleed.

Broad Beans (*Habas*): January to May

Fresh broad beans are at their cheapest in March and are widely used in northern Spain in soups and stews. The pods are long and greenish grey. Once the pod has been opened the tough outer skin can be removed to reveal a delicate green bean. Select pods that are bright in colour and a light shade of green. Reject dark-coloured samples or pods which are heavily swollen. Broad beans are at their best when they are young and tender.

Broad beans

Basic Preparation

Slit the pods along the edge and remove the beans. You can keep the pods and use them as a flavouring for soups, stews and stock. Boil the beans in salted water until tender — 2-5 minutes. Drain well and serve with a knob of butter.

Broccoli (*Brecol*): January to May

Sometimes described as 'poor man's

asparagus', broccoli is a delicious vegetable in its own right and is widely available throughout Spain. It belongs to the same family as the cauliflower. Look for bunches that are bright in colour and with no yellow tinges on the flowers. Like asparagus, broccoli heads cook much faster than the stalks. If the stems are particularly thick, trim the ends and make two crosswise cuts right up to the point where the stalk becomes quite thin. This will help the broccoli to cook evenly.

Basic Preparation

Wash the broccoli well and remove any dead or wilted leaves. Trim the ends of the stems and make crosswise slits in the ends of the thicker stems. Add the broccoli to boiling salted water so that it is completely covered and simmer for 10-15 minutes or until the stems are tender. Drain the broccoli and serve with a knob of butter. Broccoli can be cooked in bundles as for asparagus. This method is particularly suitable when the broccoli is spindly.

Brussels Sprouts (*Coles de Bruselas*): January to March

Brussels sprouts can be excellent but it is important to choose only small, hard and compact specimens which will have that characteristic nutty flavour when cooked. This can sometimes be a little difficult, as both large, overblown sprouts and smaller, compact samples, are often mixed in together.

Cabbage (*Col*): January to May

There are two varieties of cabbage commonly available in Spain. The pale-green type which is solid, with a tight head, and the darker-leaved, pointed variety, which is loosely packed. Cabbage is at its cheapest in April.

31

Celery (*Apio*)

Celery is quite widely available and the quality is generally good. Choose celery that is firm and unblemished and with leaves that look fresh and green.

Lettuce (*Lechuga*)

Lettuce is available all the year round but the quality is variable. Iceberg lettuce, or a similar variety is available at a price, but with ordinary, 'loose-leafed' lettuce try and buy smaller samples, discard the outer leaves and use only the hearts and the surrounding leaves.

Mushrooms (*Champiñones*): January to March

Both the smaller 'button' variety and the large 'field' type are available. The latter always has a better flavour. Wild mushrooms are available in the autumn in parts of northern Spain and the islands and they are quite superb. Don't attempt to pick your own wild mushrooms unless you are really sure you know what you are doing.

Onions

Onions (*Cebollas*): all year

The Spanish onion is larger than most other varieties. It has a brown skin, sometimes tinged with purple, and purple-white flesh. It is quite mild and sweet in flavour and is used extensively in Spain as a major ingredient in salads. Stronger-flavoured globe onions are also available and are better for long, slow cooking. They are usually smaller with a fairly uniformly coloured brown skin.

Peas (*Guisantes*): February to June

Spanish peas are not as good as their British or American counterparts. But if you choose pods which are brightly coloured they will be fresh. Dark green or swollen, puffy pods, will be poor quality.

Peppers

Peppers (*Pimientos*): September to February (red), December to October (green)

Perhaps one of the most popular vegetables in Spain for salads, as a cooked vegetable, or as an ingredient for stews. The red, green and yellow peppers are all the same variety. Their colour simply indicates the stage of ripeness they have reached. They have a sweet, mild flavour and the red pepper is sometimes dried and then ground to make paprika. The smaller red and green chilli peppers are more elongated and these are very strong in flavour. The seeds of these peppers are extremely hot and should be removed if a milder flavour is required. Look for peppers that are firm with unwrinkled and unblemished skin. Reject any dull or soft samples.

Potatoes (*Patatas*): all year

The potato is one of the most important food plants in the world and is a staple food in the Spanish diet. It was the Spanish who first introduced the potato to Europe after their conquest of South

33

America in the late 16th century. The potato was then a little-known, wild plant growing on the lower slopes of the Andes. Most main dishes in Spanish restaurants are accompanied by fried potatoes and they are a key ingredient in *tortilla Español* (Spanish omelette). The quality of potatoes is generally good and both the red- and the white-skinned types are available.

Spinach (*Espinaca*): December to May

Spinach is easily obtainable in central and northern Spain. Choose crisp, well-developed leaves with a good strong overall colour. Reject straggly or limp leaves.

Sweet Potatoes (*Boniatos or Batatas*): all year

The sweet potato bears no relation to the ordinary potato. The soft-fleshed variety is most commonly available in Spain and is particularly popular in the Canary Islands. Sweet potatoes can be boiled, sautéed, deep-fried or stewed. They are at their best when baked in their jackets and served with butter. Select specimens that are smooth and firm with no wounds in the skin.

Basic Preparation

Peel the potatoes and cut the large ones into smaller, uniform sizes. Put the potatoes in a saucepan and add salt and enough cold water to cover. Bring the water to the boil rapidly, cover the pan and simmer for 30-40 minutes or until the vegetable is tender when pierced with the point of a sharp knife.

Tomatoes (*Tomates*): January to October

The tomato is one of the most widely used vegetables in Spain and a number of varieties are available. Tiny, sweet varieties are cultivated in the Canary Islands, although the larger tomato, with irregularly shaped ridges is generally the most popular. This type is often tinged with green but it is still quite ripe and is excellent for salads. With the larger tomatoes, it is advisable to skin them first. Immerse them briefly in boiling water, pierce the skin with the point of a sharp knife and you will find that the skin will peel away very easily.

FRUIT AND VEGETABLES

Vocabulary

Apples	*Manzanas*
Apricots	*Albaricoques*
Avocado Pears	*Aguacates*
Bananas	*Plátanos/Bananas*
Blackberries	*Zarzamoras*
Blackcurrants	*Grosellas Negras*
Cherries	*Guindas* or *Cerezas*
Custard Apple	*Chirimoya*
Figs	*Higos*
Grapefruit	*Pomelo*
Grapes	*Uvas*
Lemons	*Limones*
Limes	*Limas*
Mangoes	*Mangos*
Melon	*Melón*
Oranges	*Naranjas*
Peaches	*Melocotones*
Pears	*Peras*
Persimmons	*Nísperos*
Pineapple	*Piña*
Plums	*Ciruelas*
Pomegranates	*Granadas*
Raspberries	*Frambuesas*
Redcurrants	*Grosellas Rojas*
Tangerines	*Mandarinas*
Artichokes	*Alcachofas*
Asparagus	*Espárrago*
Aubergine (Eggplant)	*Berenjena*
Beetroot	*Remolachas*

Broad Beans	*Habas*
Broccoli	*Brecol*
Brussels Sprouts	*Coles de Bruselas*
Cabbage	*Col*
Celery	*Apio*
Lettuce	*Lechuga*
Mushrooms	*Champiñones*
Onions	*Cebollas*
Peas	*Guisantes*
Peppers	*Pimientos*
Potatoes	*Patatas*
Spinach	*Espinaca*
Sweet Potatoes	*Boniatos* or *Batatas*
Tomatoes	*Tomates*

Phrases

How much is this?	*Cuánto cuesta esto?*
How much is this a kilo?	*Cuánto cuesta por un kilo?*
Please write it down	*Escríbamelo por favor*
Do you have any …?	*Tiene usted …?*
No more, thanks	*Nada mas, gracias*
I would like a …	*Quisiera un …*
I'd like that	*Quisiera ese*
What is this?	*Que es esto?*
I'd like … kilo(s) of	*Quisiera … kilo(s) de*
Is it ripe?	*Es maduro?*

4

MEATS, POULTRY AND GAME

POULTRY

Chicken (*Pollo*)

Don't be fooled by Spanish chickens. They may appear less plump — even scrawny in comparison to our birds — but they almost always have a better flavour and texture. More often than not, they are bred on small farms and have the run of the yard, and this helps to breed birds with less fat and considerably more flavour. Battery farming of chickens is not a widespread practice in Spain. You will notice that the skin is darker, quite often a deep shade of yellow. This, again, is the result of more natural breeding methods and should be welcomed.

Chicken is very economical and versatile, with prices slightly lower than those in Britain. When you buy your chicken in a butcher's shop or in the market it will almost always be sold to you complete with head, feet and intestines and the price charged will be for the total weight. Butchers will happily gut and clean the bird and will then include the feet, head and innards with your purchase. Chicken pieces are easily obtainable and butchers will always quarter a chicken at your request. Ask for *pollo*, the young male bird, for roasting, and *gallina*, the older hen-bird, for stewing or boiling.

Frozen chicken and frozen chicken pieces are also available in the supermarkets and it is often possible to buy whole, spit-roasted chicken. This will cost you more — usually around 30 per cent.

Turkey (*Pavo*)

Turkeys are not farmed intensively in Spain and it is unusual to see the plump, broad-breasted 'white' variety we buy at home. In Spain you will see turkeys with much darker skins, known as 'bronze' turkeys. Again, the flavour is far superior.

GAME

Duck (*Pato*)

Ducks do not thrive well in hot, dry climates, and, although it is possible to buy duck in the Spanish markets, they are not usually as plump and succulent as those we buy here.

Goose (*Oca*)

It is rare to see goose on the menu, or in the markets of southern Spain. Like ducks, geese are not so well suited to the climate, although they are bred in northern Spain. Goose is the main ingredient for a delicious Catalan recipe, *oca con peras* — goose with pears.

Partridge (*Perdíz*)

The Spanish are fanatical hunters and the mountainous nature of much of the Spanish peninsula provides an ideal habitat for small game. Partridge was once the most commonly eaten game bird in Spain but intensive hunting over the years has seriously depleted numbers. It is still quite widely available and is a speciality in the Balearic Islands. Partridge, together with most other Spanish game, is hung for a long time. The Spanish like their game 'high', so check before you buy if you prefer a less gamey flavour.

Quail (*Cordoníz*)

As with partridge, quail have also been intensively hunted and they are now considered a luxury dish. They are quite superb when prepared the Spanish way — wrapped in a vine leaf and served on a slice of fried bread. Quail should not be hung and should be eaten as soon as possible after they are killed.

Rabbit (*Conejo*)

Not one of the most popular meats here, rabbit is widely used in Spanish recipes and often to great effect. Generally speaking, rabbit can be treated in exactly the same way as chicken, but there are recipes particularly suited to the stronger flavour of rabbit meat. Rabbit is obtainable in markets and in some butcher's shops. Ask the butcher to joint your rabbit into suitable pieces for stewing, frying or grilling.

MEATS

Beef (*Carne*) and Veal (*Ternera*)

If you are looking forward to juicy cuts of beef, you will be disappointed. Shortage of suitable grazing for large animals means that cows are usually killed far younger in Spain and the result is a cross between beef and veal. The meat is not hung for as long as it is in Britain, so it is sensible to buy your meat a few days before you need it, unless you are using it for stewing. Here, longer, slower cooking will help to tenderise the meat. Having said this, I should point out that the flavour of both Spanish beef and veal can be quite excellent. Much depends on the cut of the meat and on the age of the animal when slaughtered.

Beef and veal is graded into two main classifications — first by age, and, second, by the part of the carcass the cut comes from. *Ternera de Avila* or *ternera lechál* refers to the youngest meat — broadly equivalent to the white veal available here. *Anojo* is approximately one year old — still veal in our terms. *Ternera* and *vacuno* are from animals aged between two and three years old and so, in spite of the name, are really beef. Finally, the oldest type of meat, *lidia*, is from bulls killed in the ring.

Unfortunately it does not become any less confusing when choosing cuts of meat. Fillet is called *solomillo*; *lomo* refers to the ribs, both sirloin and top-ribs; *primera A* is roughly equivalent to topside, silverside and rump; *primera B* covers cuts from the shoulder as well as part of the neck; *segunda* is taken from the shin and the flank; and *tercera*, the lowest grade of meat, includes the brisket, neck and tail. Spanish butchers will always be happy to mince your meat for you or cut it into suitable pieces for stewing.

Lamb (*Cordero*)

Lamb is eaten much younger here than at home and is almost always of excellent quality. Prices are similar to those we pay at home. Lamb is often so young that it has been reared only on its mother's milk and is known as *lechál* lamb, or milk lamb — a traditional Easter speciality with quite a different flavour from that of the lamb we know.

Lamb cuts are similar to those we buy here but the proportion of bone to flesh of such familiar cuts as leg and shoulder is much greater. Because the animals are so much smaller than at home, when you order leg of lamb in a restaurant, that is exactly what you get — a whole leg. Again, this is because lamb is killed so much younger. As with beef, there is a grading system applied to lamb but it is comparatively simple, and again based on the age of the animal. *Cordero lechál* is lamb that is not more than one month old and *cordero pascual* refers to any lamb which is older than this.

Offal (*Menudillos*)

Spanish housewives are very thrifty; nothing is allowed to go to waste. Liver (*higado*) and hearts (*corazón*) are easily obtainable. Kidneys (*riñones*) are the main ingredient in a classic Spanish dish, kidneys in sherry (*Riñones jerez*). Offal represents excellent value for money and can be purchased, frozen, in most supermarkets.

Pork (*Carne de Cerdo*)

Like chicken, pork represents one of the best buys. It is widely used in Spanish cooking and pork products are an everyday staple in Spanish kitchens. One of the most delicious dishes is roast suckling pig — a whole baby pig roasted to crisp tender perfection. It may not be practical, with limited cooking facilities, to attempt roast suckling pig yourself, but try to find this superb dish in local restaurants. It will be well worth the effort and the money, for it does cost a lot. Pork is cut in much the same way in Spain as it is here and you should have no trouble recognising the joints.

MEAT PRODUCTS

Bacon (*Tocino*)

Almost all bacon sold in Spain is streaky. Having said this, many of the supermarkets and hypermarkets in the tourist areas now stock vacuum-packed back bacon. It is mainly imported, and this is reflected in the price. It is far better to buy bacon in butcher's shops or on the meat stalls in the markets. If you prefer your bacon not too salty, then look for a joint that is not too dark red in colour. Generally speaking, the lighter the colour, the milder the flavour. Spanish butchers will slice bacon to any thickness you want.

Ham (*Jamón*)

Wind-dried ham is a famous, but expensive, Spanish delicacy. You will see an enormous variety of hams, from different regions of Spain, each employing a slightly different curing method, hanging in bars and markets.

They are quite different from anything we have here, and, with their brown, leathery skins and dark red meat veined with fat, they look rather unappetising to the uninitiated. This ham is usually sliced wafer-thin and eaten on its own as a *tapa*, or as an hors d'oeuvre. It is sometimes used as an ingredient in soups, stews and omelettes. It has a slightly salty flavour and is often quite chewy. However, it is well worth trying in spite of its high price.

English-style ham is available and you should ask for York Ham — *jamón York*. *Jamón serrano*, or mountain ham, is

Ham

cured in huge caverns high in the mountains. *Jamón de bellotas* — acorn ham — comes from pigs that graze beneath orchards of ilex or evergreen oak. In the autumn the acorns drop and the eager pigs, having gorged themselves, are whisked off to play their part in making this delicious ham — a gourmet's delight.

Patés (*Pates*)

There are plenty of different varieties to choose from. Many are made from pork and chicken livers although the game patés are possibly the finest. Once again, regional and local variations make it impossible to list specific types. Buy small quantities of two or three different types until you find one that you particularly like.

Sausages (*Salchichas*)

There are so many regional variations and specialities, as well as local variations within the regions, that it is simply not practical to list all the types of sausage available. A quick glance to the rafters in covered markets and some bars will reveal an astounding and utterly confusing array of red, black and 'white' sausages hanging in between the hams. Sausages are eaten as *tapas*, as a main course and are frequently used as an ingredient for stews.

One of the most popular types of sausage is *chorizo*. This is a general term for spiced sausage, but there are hundreds of different types available. They all have the basic ingredients of pork, peppers, garlic and salt and most of them are coarse-textured and can be very chewy and spicy. They vary in diameter and length. You will have to try a few different types to find one that is to your taste. They can be very fatty, and it is advisable to use this type in cooking. *Chorizo* should be sliced thinly for eating as a *tapa* snack or hors d'hoeuvre. When buying sausage in a market or shop, be sure to ask if it can be eaten raw (*crudo*), or if it must be cooked.

Morcilla, or 'blood' sausage, is another variety which is available in a number of different disguises. The basic ingredients are pork blood and fat, onions and spices. *Morcilla* has a marked smoky flavour and is excellent fried as an accompaniment to eggs.

Butifarra is another pork-based sausage — a speciality of both Mallorca and Catalonia, though it is widely available throughout Spain. The small, thinner versions are known as *butifarrones*. The basic ingredients are pork, fat, salt, pepper, garlic, cinnamon and cloves. *Butifarra negra* is similar, but with the addition of pig's blood. Generally this sausage is used as an ingredient for soups and stews.

Salami is commonly available and, depending on the region it comes from, is often milder in flavour than the Italian product.

Another Mallorcan speciality is *sobresada*. This is quite different from most other Spanish sausages and has a soft, spreading consistency. It is made from pork, pork liver, tripe and paprika. A variety of *sobresada*, known as *longaniza*, is similar to British sausage in size and is made from lean pork, garlic and paprika. As with our sausages, this type must always be cooked.

British-style sausages can be obtained in supermarkets but are not popular with Spaniards.

MEAT, POULTRY, GAME AND MEAT PRODUCTS

Vocabulary

Bacon	*Tocino*
Beef	*Carne (de vaca)*
Chicken	*Pollo*
Duck	*Pato*
Goose	*Oca*
Ham	*Jamón*
Lamb	*Cordero*
Offal	*Menudillos*
Partridge	*Perdíz*
Paté	*Pate*

Pork	*Carne de cerdo*
Quail	*Cordoníz*
Rabbit	*Conejo*
Sausages	*Salchichas*
Turkey	*Pavo*
Veal	*Ternera*

Phrases

How much is this?	*Cuánto cuesta esto?*
How much is this per kilo?	*Cuánto cuesta por un kilo?*
Please write it down	*Escríbamelo por favor*
Do you have any ...?	*Tiene usted ...?*
No more, thanks	*Nada mas, gracias*
I would like a ...	*Quisiera un ...*
I'd like that	*Quisiera ese*
What is this?	*Qué es esto?*
I'd like ... kilo(s) of	*Quisiera ... kilo(s) de*
A bigger piece, please	*Un trozo/pedazo mas grande por favor*
A smaller piece, please	*Un trozo/pedazo mas chico por favor*
Please mince it	*Puede usted picarlo por favor*
Please cut it	*Puede usted cortarlo por favor*
Please slice it	*Puede usted cortar en lonjas por favor*
Please clean/gut it	*Puede usted limpiarlo*
I'd like some game	*Quisiera carne de Caza*
Can I eat this raw?	*Se puede comer crudo?*
Is this cooked?	*Está cocido esto?*
I would like ... kilo(s) of	*Quisiera ... kilo(s) de ...*
belly	*panceta*
chops	*chuletas*
fillet	*solomillo*
fore-ribs	*lomo alto*
heart	*corazón*
kidneys	*riñones*
liver	*higado*
loin	*lomobajo*
mince	*carne picada*
ribs	*costillas*
shoulder	*brazuelo*
sweetbreads	*criadillas*
suckling pig	*cochinillo*
tripe	*callos*

I'd like some chicken ...	*Quisiera ...*
breast	*pechugo de pollo*
leg	*muslo de pollo*

5
FISH AND SEAFOOD

FISH (*PESCADO*)

Spain has the longest coastline in Europe, bordering the Mediterranean, the Bay of Biscay and the Atlantic Ocean. It is hardly surprising, therefore, that fish plays such an important part in the Spanish diet. The Spanish are extremely fussy about the freshness of their fish and will disdain anything that has not been caught that very day. It can be quite difficult to tell if the fish is thoroughly fresh, as most fishmarkets constantly sluice their produce with water to keep it cool and clean. This has the effect of making the fish glisten and appear fresher than perhaps it may be. So, take a tip from the Spanish housewife and look for fish with clear, shining eyes and flesh which is firm and smells of the sea. It should spring back into shape when pressed gently with the fingers. Nobody will mind, or be surprised, if you do this.

Mostly the Spanish like to eat their fish very small. This is particularly true in southern Spain where their mastery with the frying pan is ideally suited to the preparation of mounds of tiny fish cooked to crisp perfection and brought to the table still sizzling hot. You would recognise many of the tiny fish on sale if they had been allowed to grow to full maturity. Sole, or hake, for instance are often eaten when they are only a few centimetres in length. This is not to say that larger fish are not available. Most markets display wicked-looking swordfish and huge blue-black tuna as well as the more familiar species such as mullet, mackerel and salmon.

With the exception of large fish, over 5 kg in weight, all fresh fish is sold complete with head and innards. The price shown is for the total weight. The fishmonger will always clean the fish for you and skin it if required. With such an abundance of fresh fish, it would seem criminal to buy it frozen. In the markets you will see some fish displayed on beds of ice. These fish are only partially frozen and often already have their heads removed. They are still a good buy, but you should make sure they are still absolutely fresh.

Packets of frozen fish can be purchased in supermarkets and the quality is usually excellent. The Spanish, however, seem to have the same problem grading their fish as they do grading their fruit and vegetables. You will find an assortment of sizes in the packet and this can make planning a meal a little problematic.

There is also a wide selection of canned fish and many of the varieties are exactly the same as you buy in Britain — tinned tuna fish, sardines, herrings, mackerel, etc. The fish is usually packed in oil or tomato sauce and occasionally in brine. If you enjoy a hot, spicy flavour look out for fish in piquant sauce (*pil-pil*). Be careful, though: this sauce contains chilli powder. Prices are quite reasonable and a few tins of fish are a useful addition to your larder. Use them to pad out lunchtime salads or as snacks on their own

Anchovy, Baby (*Boquerón*)

The anchovy is a member of the herring family and is similar to this fish in colour and shape, although rarely more than 7 cm long. Anchovy is very plentiful in Spain and extremely popular, especially in the south. I had never tried fresh anchovies before I visited Spain. They are a rare treat, bearing little relation to the tinned, heavily salted variety we buy here.

Basic Preparation

If the anchovies are uniformly small, wash them thoroughly, dredge with seasoned flour and fry in very hot oil. Toss the pan constantly to keep the fish moving and ensure even cooking. About 3-5 minutes should be sufficient. Cut off the heads and eat whole with lemon juice. If the fish are large, they should be gutted and the heads removed before cooking.

Anglerfish (*Rape*)

Don't be put off by the grotesque appear-ance of this fish. It is one of the most

popular in Spain and its flesh has a similar flavour to lobster. It can easily be
identified by its enormous gaping mouth
and milky white underside. Sometimes
the fish-stalls turn the fish over and
display it belly side up so as not to put off
the customers. Buy it in thick steaks and
bake with just a little butter or oil and
seasoning for about 20 minutes. Serve
hot or cold with a piquant sauce or
lemon juice.

Bass (Stone) (*Cherna*)

A large, dark-coloured fish, sometimes as
much as 120 cm long, although the type
most often found in Mediterranean markets is much smaller. It is usually sold in
steaks or fillets. It has a good flavour, with
firm, meaty flesh. It is outstanding baked,
grilled or fried.

Bream (Red) (*Besugo*)

This fish is a member of the large sea
bream family. It can be identified by its
reddish-grey colour and a large, black
spot on its shoulder. The younger specimens are quite different, with blue spots
dotted all over their backs. The adult
specimens can be up to 50 cm long, while
the 'baby' *besugo* is less than half that
size. They can be grilled, fried or baked.

Bream (Sea) (*Pagro*)

Another member of the prolific bream
family. It has rosy tints on its back and
sides and a white tip on its tail. It is good
cut into steaks and fried, or stuffed and
baked.

Brill (*Remól*)

If you like turbot you will love *remol*. This
fish varies in colour from dark brown to
green-brown on the upper side and has a
good flavour and delicate flesh. It is best
baked with wine and served with a
mayonnaise-based sauce.

Chanquette (no translation)

This tiny fish is similar to whitebait and very popular in Spain. It has a transparent appearance and should be washed thoroughly under running water, rolled in seasoned flour and deep-fried for about 20-30 seconds. Serve with lemon wedges.

Gilthead (*Dorada*)

Another member of the bream family, this fish has a silver skin with faint golden stripes. It is considered to be the finest type of bream and it does have an excellent flavour. It is very good baked in white wine and herbs.

Grouper (*Mero*)

Don't be put off by the hideous aspect of this monster. It can be reddish or yellow-brown in colour with darker, cloudy patches or with a dark grey back and white underside. The flesh is firm with mild, delicate flavour and is blissfully free of small bones. *Mero* can be grilled, baked whole, or cut into steaks. It is best served cold with a lightly flavoured sauce.

Hake (*Merluza*)

Merluza is very plentiful in Spain and very good value for money. Larger varieties, up to 120 cm in length, are to be found on the Atlantic coast, while smaller hake are more common in Mediterranean fishmarkets. It has a silvery skin and tender, firm white flesh. In some southern Spanish fishmarkets, the large Atlantic variety are on sale and may be partially frozen. *Merluza* is easily filleted and can be cooked in a number of ways — by poaching, grilling, baking, steaming or frying. This fish is equally good eaten hot or cold.

Mackerel Family (*Estornino/Caballa*)

The mackerel is a 'blue' fish with meaty flesh and a high oil content. It is full of flavour and very economical. *Caballa* can be recognised by its long body, silver underside and blue/green stripes. This fish can be baked, grilled or fried.

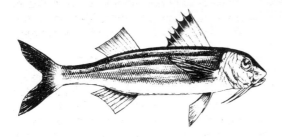

Red mullet

Mullet (Red) (*Salmonete*)

There are two main types on sale. The *salmonete roca*, with a maximum length of 40 cm and recognisable by stripes on the first dorsal fin (and, occasionally, yellow stripes on its flanks), has an overall reddish colour. The smaller type, *salmonete de fango*, is rarely larger than 25 cm and is a paler red. Both varieties should be grilled, fried or baked whole. Gut these fish after cooking, not before. This will make a considerable difference to the flavour.

Palometa (no translation)

This fish is not available here but it is inexpensive and very good with firm, white, pleasantly-flavoured flesh. It can be baked or grilled, but is best filleted and fried in oil.

Plaice (*Platija*)

This fish is more common in northern Spain and is brown or greyish in colour with small, reddish spots. It is often caught much smaller than is the case here and is delicious fried.

Salmon (*Salmón*)

Expensive and similar to British salmon. Can be grilled, fried or baked.

Sardine

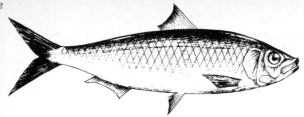

Sardines (*Sardinas*)

One of the best buys in Spanish fish-markets. Wash thoroughly and, leaving the heads on, deep-fry in a light batter. For larger sardines, grill with a little oil and seasoning.

Sole (*Lenguado*)

Sole is a member of the flatfish family. It is elongated and oval in shape and varies in colour from dark brownish-grey to reddish-brown. Although the *lenguado* found in Spanish fishmarkets will not have the wonderful, subtle flavour of our Dover sole, it is still quite delicious and the smaller-sized fish are very good value. *Lenguado* can be as heavy as 2 kg in weight right down to the small-fry at less than 15 cm long. Frying baby sole is particularly popular in southern Spain. You should try them if you get the opportunity.

Basic Preparation

Prepare the baby *lenguado* by skinning them and removing their fins with a sharp knife or scissors. Dip the fish in egg and breadcrumbs or seasoned flour and fry for a few minutes. The larger, adult fish can be baked, grilled or fried.

Swordfish (*Pez Espada*)

You shouldn't have a great deal of trouble identifying this brute. It can be as big as 4 m in length, although you will frequently see just a large section of the fish on a

slab in the fishmarkets. The flesh is pinkish, close-grained and meaty. It has a
really superb flavour and is best simply
grilled or fried in a little oil or butter and
lemon juice. Ask for steaks about 2 cm
thick. It is quite expensive, but worth
every peseta.

Trout (*Trucha*)

There are a number of fresh and sea-
water varieties available. They are all
similar to the types on sale here and can
be prepared in exactly the same way.

Trout (Sea) (*Baila*)

Sea trout is the same family as sea bass
and can be treated in much the same
way. It has small, dark spots on either
side of its body and a delicious, delicately-
flavoured pale pink or white flesh. It is
most common in southern Spain. The
smaller fish, about 1 kg in weight, have
a better flavour and texture. They can be
baked in the oven with a little white wine,
seasoning and herbs; smaller fish are
excellent either grilled or fried.

Tuna (*Atún*)

This huge fish reaches up to 7 m in
length. It has a dark blue back with firm,
meaty flesh. Buy your tuna in steaks and
grill or bake in white wine.

Whiting (*Pescadilla*)

These are usually sold much smaller than
here. They have only one bone and are
ideal for deep-frying whole. Dip them in
seasoned flour and cook for about 2
minutes.

SHELLFISH (*MARISCOS*)

The price of most shellfish, with some
exceptions, is really quite high. This
does not appear to deter the Spanish
who are passionately fond of this seafood

and consume enormous quantities of it. The fishmarkets offer a huge variety of uncooked shellfish, and in most towns you will find *mariscerías*, shops specialising in cooked seafood.

There are many different varieties of shellfish and it would be impossible to try and list them all. If you would like to know more, it would be well worth investing in a copy of Alan Davidson's superb book, *Mediterranean Seafood*, which not only describes the fish in considerable detail, but provides excellent line drawings to help you identify the more unusual varieties.

Although we have included a number of recipes using shellfish, the quality of the fish is so good that justice can best be done to it with simple cooking methods and the accompaniment of a lightly garlic-flavoured sauce.

Frozen shellfish is available in larger supermarkets and you can buy a good range of tinned varieties. Neither have that delicious, straight-from-the-sea flavour of market-bought fish.

If you buy your shellfish live from the market, there are a number of ways of killing it. Which method is most humane is a debatable point. Some experts say that the immersion of a lobster, for instance, in cold water, bringing it gradually to the boil over a low heat, is the best method, while others say it should be plunged into rapidly boiling water. In some cases — crab, for example — inserting a pin into the central nervous system is the quickest and most effective means. Ask the fishmonger to show you the correct spot.

Shellfish is delicious and you should try as many different types as possible. But do make sure to choose fresh produce and, particularly in the case of shellfish, follow the instructions carefully and ensure that you discard any that are even slightly suspect.

PRAWNS (*GAMBAS*)

Prawns are frequently sold ready-cooked, but in the fishmarkets you will buy them raw. There are a number of types available, varying in colour and size. All prawns turn pink when they are cooked.

Camarón or *Quisquilla Camarón*

These are the smallest type of prawn, often no bigger than 5 cm in length. They are greyish-pink in colour and semi-translucent, with dark spots. They are the type used for dishes such as potted shrimp. They are extremely fiddly to shell and the small amount of meat they offer is not really worth the effort.

Carabinero

A much larger prawn, sometimes as much as 20 cm long and brilliant red in colour.

Gambas

Although this is the generic Spanish name for prawn it also applies to a specific variety, which can make things very complicated. It is never much bigger than 15 cm in length and has a rosy-pink colour.

Giant prawn

Langostino

Another large prawn, this type is brown with a reddish tinge. It has an elongated head and 'beak'.

Basic Preparation

This method is appropriate, with certain

55

adjustments for size, for any type of prawn. Wash the prawns thoroughly under running water and drain off. Fill a large saucepan about a quarter full with water (sea-water is ideal) and bring rapidly to the boil over a high heat. Add seasoning if fresh water is used and, if you wish, a slice of onion and a parsley stalk. Put the prawns into the boiling water. They should be just covered, so add more water if necessary. Reduce the heat and simmer for 5-10 minutes or until they are tender. Be careful not to over-cook the prawns as they will take on a rather unpleasant, rubbery texture. Prawns can be served hot or cold but not chilled, as this impairs the flavour. To shell cooked prawns, grasp the fish in the middle and pull firmly, first at the tail end and then at the head. You will find that both come away quite easily.

Lobster (*Langosta*)

Lobsters are large shellfish belonging to the crab family. A fully grown European lobster can weigh as much as 4 kg. For eating purposes, however, lobsters weighing no more than 1 kg are best, as the flesh of larger specimens tends to be rather coarse. Lobster enthusiasts argue over whether the male or female lobster is best. The 'cock' lobster has larger claws and they contain very tender flesh, while its tail is smaller, with flesh that is full of flavour; the 'hen' lobster has the roe, which is a blackish-green colour when

Lobster

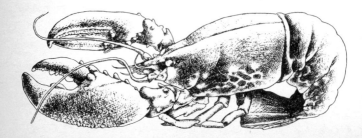

56

raw, turning to bright red when cooked. The roe is used as a garnish or flavouring and is good in soups. Live lobsters are bluish-black in colour and sometimes tinged with green or purple. If you are buying live lobster, make sure it is still active. If it is behaving in a sluggish fashion, or not moving at all, don't buy. When cooked, lobsters turn bright red in colour.

Basic Preparation

Method 1 Immerse the lobster, head first, into rapidly boiling water and cook for 20 minutes.

Method 2 Place the lobster in a large saucepan and cover with salted water. Bring the saucepan to the boil over a very low heat and then cook for 20 minutes.

When the lobster has cooled, twist off the large claws and crack them open with a small hammer. Set aside for decoration. Using a very sharp knife, split the lobster lengthways down the middle. Remove the sac, which you will find near the head, and the thin, dark gut running just below the surface. Don't remove the creamy substance or the green liver. Arrange the lobster on a serving dish and garnish with the claws, parsley and lemon wedges.

Lobster is also delicious grilled. Having killed the lobster, as outlined in Method 1 or 2, take a sharp knife and slit in two, lengthwise. Remove the sac and gut. Brush with oil and butter and season well. Place the lobster, shell side down, under a high grill and cook for approximately 15 minutes.

Bogavante

This is the largest variety of lobster, in fact the only true lobster.

Cigalas

This is the smallest of the lobster group and is more commonly known here as the Dublin Bay prawn or scampi. It is rarely longer than 25 cm and either grey-pink or pink. Cook for 8-10 minutes in boiling salted water and serve with melted butter or garlic mayonnaise.

Langosta

Further confusion: yes, this is the generic Spanish word for lobster but it is also applied specifically to the spiny lobster — a clawless variety with a reddish-brown body with yellow and white markings. Its maximum length is 50 cm. Spiny lobster is widely available throughout the Mediterranean coastal resorts.

Cigarra

The *cigarra*, or flat lobster, is easily identifiable by its very short legs and knobbly shell.

MOLLUSCS

There are a wide variety of molluscs on sale in Spain. Many of them you will recognise. The following is an outline of some of the more popular varieties.

Globito or Chipirón

This is a small variety of cuttlefish, rarely longer than 4 cm; they are often sold fried and ready to eat. If you buy them raw, ask the fishmonger to extract the small bone and the ink sac. Wash them well. Dry them and deep-fry for about 8 minutes.

Squid (*Calamares*)

The squid is similar to octopus in texture and flavour. To clean squid, remove and discard the fine, membrane-like skin and the triangular fins. Take hold of the head and pull it away from the body. Wash the squid thoroughly, inside and out, under running water. Dredge with seasoned flour and deep-fry for about 5 to 8 minutes.

Octopus (*Pulpo/Pulpito*)

The octopus has eight arms or tentacles — hence the name. Its flesh has a rather rubbery texture. All parts of the octopus, except the eyes, beak and internal organs (all of which should be removed) are edible. A great delicacy, octopus can be bought ready-bashed; you will often see the fisherman enthusiastically beating the living daylights out of the poor thing on the rocks.

Basic Preparation

Preparing an octopus for the pot is rather a strenuous exercise. Hold the octopus under running water, and using a very sharp knife, cut out the eyes, beak and internal organs. Be careful not to pierce the ink sac. Turn the head inside out and remove the membranes. Discard the yellowish-coloured pouch and the ink sac — that is, if you do not wish to cook the octopus in its own ink. Squeeze the tentacles all the way down to remove any unwanted sand or grit lodged inside and then rinse the octopus thoroughly. Boil the octopus for five minutes in salted water. Drain and rinse in cold water. Cut off the ends of the tentacles and peel off the skin. Wash again in cold water. Take a wooden mallet and beat the octopus vigorously for at least five minutes. Rinse again. The octopus can now be cooked, if you have enough energy left to eat it. Octopus can be stewed or fried.

Almejas

This is a general term for clams. They can vary from about 1 cm to 3 cm in diameter. The shell colour can be tan or grey and sometimes bears a darker mark in the centre. *Almejas* can be eaten either raw with lemon juice or cooked. In either case, wash them thoroughly under plenty of running water to remove any mud or grit. Discard any that are not tightly shut or do not close when sharply tapped on the top of the shell. Soak for an hour in lightly salted water and then drain in a colander. Put half an inch of water in a large saucepan and add the *almejas*. Cover the saucepan tightly and place over a high heat. Cook for 5-10 minutes, stirring occasionally, until all the *almejas* have opened. Discard any that remain closed.

Winkles (*Bigaros*)

Winkles can vary considerably in size. Wash the winkles thoroughly and soak for 10 minutes in clean water. Wash again. Drain and cook in boiling salted water for 20 minutes.

Whelks (*Busanos*)

This small mollusc is quite common in Spain and looks exactly the same as the type available here. Wash the whelks thoroughly under running water and ensure that you remove all the sand. Bring a saucepan of sea-water or salted water to the boil and add the whelks. Simmer for half an hour. Drain well. Use a pin to extract the flesh from the shell.

Conchas Finas

This is a large clam, sometimes as big as 10cm across, with a red/brown shell and dark lines running all the way round. They are usually eaten raw and you will find live *conchas finas* in the fishmarkets. The shells should be slightly open, with a little pink flesh protruding. Give the shell a sharp tap and the 'tongue' should withdraw and the shell close. If this does not happen, don't buy.

Oreja de Mar

Oreja de mar is an ear-shaped mollusc containing white flesh. The inside of the shell is pearlised, while the outside is rough-surfaced and greyish or brown. The flesh should be tenderised by beating with a wooden mallet or the side of the rolling pin. The *oreja de mar* can be eaten raw, but is delicious sautéed rapidly in a little oil and garlic.

Scallops (*Peregrinas*)

You will recognise this mollusc type as the variety commonly used for the famous dish, *Coquille St. Jacques*. The edible parts are the white muscle and the orange/yellow-coloured roe. Scallops are often sold already opened. But, if this is not the case, wash the shells thoroughly and either pry them open with a knife or leave them in a warm place where they will open of their own accord. Take a sharp, pointed knife and cut away the flesh, discarding the black, gristly fibre. The shells may be kept for serving the cooked scallops in. Scallops may be boiled or fried. To boil, simmer gently in salted water for 8-10 minutes until the flesh is firm. To fry, soak in olive oil and lemon juice for about half an hour. Coat them with egg and breadcrumbs or batter and fry until golden brown — approximately 6-8 minutes.

Oysters (*Ostras*)

Not widely available in the south, this highly prized mollusc is more common in northern Spain and the islands although it is never cheap. Discard any oysters that are not tightly shut or do not shut when sharply tapped. If the oyster floats when placed in water it should be thrown away. Open the oysters by prying with a sharp knife. Chill them well and serve, sprinkled with lemon juice, on a bed of ice. Oysters can be fried or grilled — considered quite criminal by oyster devotees. They need only a very short cooking time. Overcooking impairs their delicate flavour and makes the flesh very rubbery.

Approximately 2-3 minutes should be more than sufficient.

Mussels (*Mejillones*)

Mejillones are excellent eaten raw, sprinkled with lemon juice. But, as with all other molluscs, you must ensure that they are fresh. Scrub the mussels thoroughly under running water and discard any that are not tightly shut, that have broken shells or that float when placed in water.

Mussels

FISH AND SEAFOOD

Vocabulary

Anchovy (Baby)	*Boquerón*
Anglerfish	*Rape*
Bass (Stone)	*Cherna*
Bream (Red)	*Besugo*
Bream (Sea)	*Pagro*
Brill	*Remól*
Cuttlefish	*Globito/Chipirón*
Clams	*Almejas/Conchas Finas/ Oreja de Mar*
Fish	*Pescado*
Gilthead	*Dorada*
Grouper	*Mero*
Hake	*Merluza*
Lobster	*Langosta*
Mackerel	*Estornino/Caballa*
Mullet (Red)	*Salmonete*
Mussels	*Mejillones*
Octopus	*Pulpo/Pulpito*
Oysters	*Ostras*
Plaice	*Platija*
Prawns	*Gambas*

Salmon	*Salmón*
Sardines	*Sardinas*
Scallops	*Peregrinas*
Sole	*Lenguado*
Squid	*Calamares*
Swordfish	*Pez Espada*
Trout	*Trucha*
Trout (Sea)	*Baila*
Tuna	*Atún*
Whelks	*Busanos*
Whiting	*Pescadilla*
Winkles	*Bigaros*

Phrases

How much is this?	*Cuanto cuesta esto?*
How much is this per kilo?	*Cuanto cuesta por un kilo?*
Please write it down	*Escríbamelo por favor*
Do you have any ...?	*Tiene usted ...?*
No more, thanks	*Nada mas, gracias*
I would like a ...	*Quisiera un ...*
I'd like that	*Quisiera ese*
What is this?	*Qué es esto?*
I'd like ... kilo(s) of	*Quisiera ... kilo(s) de*
Please slice it	*Puede usted cortar en lonjas por favor*
Please clean/gut it	*Puede usted limpiarlo por favor*
Is this ready to cook?	*Es esto preparado para cocinar?*

6

HERBS, SPICES, SUNDRIES AND STAPLES

Many herbs — rosemary, oregano, sage, thyme and marjoram, for instance — grow wild in Spain. Although the use of herbs in cooking is not as lavish here as it is in France, they are still widely employed in many different dishes. If you are only staying in Spain for a short period of time, of course, picking your own herbs and drying them for use in cooking is not really a practical proposition. A wide range of dried herbs can be purchased in little screw-top jars from most supermarkets and you will often find herb and spice stalls located in the fruit and vegetable sections of the big municipal markets. Here, the herbs are sold in little dried posies or small cellophane envelopes. The only exceptions are mint, parsley and garlic, all of which are sold fresh from greengrocery stalls.

Spices are sold in much the same way and a wide variety are available, especially in southern Spain where the Moorish influence on cooking traditions is strongest.

HERBS

Basil (*Albahaca*)

Basil has a delicious, pungent, warm and slightly spicy taste. It can be used fresh or dried, but has a strong flavour so it should be applied sparingly. It is very good when sprinkled over a simple tomato salad.

Bay (*Laurel*)

The dried leaves are good as flavouring for marinades, stews, cooked tomato dishes and fish.

Coriander (*Culantro*)

Coriander seeds are aromatic and sweet with a slightly bitter edge. Crush and add sparingly to sweet and savoury food. The leaves can be used as a garnish in much the same way as parsley. It does have a stronger flavour and should be used sparingly.

Chives (*Cebollinas*)

No introduction is needed to this delicately onion-flavoured herb. Try chopping it finely and sprinkling over tomato salad or add chives to your Spanish omelette.

Dill (*Eneldo*)

Both the seeds and the leaves are used in cooking. Particularly good with fish, dill seeds have a warm, aromatic flavour rather similar to that of caraway seeds. The leaves have a more delicate taste. Add them, roughly chopped, to your fish dish before serving.

Fennel (*Hinojo*)

Fennel seeds have a distinctly aniseed flavour, slightly bitter and warm. The leaves are sweeter. Use with fish and pork and in sauces and marinades.

Garlic (*Ajo*)

Spanish garlic is milder in flavour than other varieties. It is sold in dried, powdered form, but a string of fresh garlic is cheap and much better for flavouring. You will often see garlic-sellers on the streets and, of course, it can always be purchased in the markets. Garlic can be used for almost any savoury dish and is the basic flavouring for countless traditional Spanish recipes. Many Spaniards start the day by rubbing a cut clove of garlic onto an oily piece of toast. Amaze your friends by trying this for breakfast.

Marjoram (*Mejorana*)

The flavour of the marjoram commonly available in Spain is markedly stronger than that of the marjoram grown here. It has a sweet, aromatic flavour and is excellent for salads, soups, stews, stuffings and egg dishes.

Parsley (*Perejil*)

The flat-leaved type of parsley sold in Spain has a slightly stronger flavour and coarser texture than the curly-leaved variety. It can be used, dried or fresh, in almost any savoury dish.

Rosemary (*Romero*)

This strongly-flavoured herb is available both dried and fresh. Used sparingly it has a wonderful flavour and is particularly good with lamb. Sprigs of fresh rosemary thrown onto barbecue coals give off a delightful, heady aroma. Walking in the dry hills of southern Spain, you will find the sun-baked rosemary gives off such a pungent smell that it becomes quite intoxicating.

Sage (*Salvia*)

Very good with fatty foods, this herb has a strong aromatic flavour with a slightly bitter edge. Good with veal and pork and in stuffings.

Tarragon (*Estragón*)

This herb has a subtle flavour with a sharp, bitter bite. It adds a distinctive flavour to sauces, salads, egg and fish dishes, but the flavour can dominate, so use sparingly.

Thyme (*Tomillo*)

Important in Spanish cooking, this pungent herb lives well with garlic, olives and tomatoes and can be used, either fresh or dried, in stews, soups and with poultry. Use with restraint: this herb has a very robust flavour which will survive even long, slow cooking.

Chillis

SPICES

Chilli (*Chili*)

There are a number of different varieties of chilli pepper and they can vary a great deal in strength. Dried chillis are used, together with cumin and garlic, for chilli powder. Fresh chillis can be finely chopped and added to sauces, curries and marinades. Do be careful to wash your hands thoroughly after handling fresh chillis. The juice is very strong and it will be rather painful if you get it in your eyes.

Cinnamon (*Canela*)

This spice has a delicate sweet flavour. Buy it ground or in little strips of bark. Add a pinch to puddings, cakes, hot drinks and some sauces.

Cloves (*Clavos*)

Cloves contain a highly scented oil and should be used sparingly. Cloves are not easy to grind by hand, so if you plan to use this spice, it would be sensible to have both whole and ground cloves to hand. They can be used in sweet and savoury dishes. Good when added to beef stews or used with ham and onions.

Cumin (*Comino*)

The powerful, aromatic flavour of this spice is excellent with bean stews and curries.

Nutmeg (*Nuez Moscada*)

Nutmegs can be purchased ready ground. But, ideally, whole nutmeg should be bought and then grated finely, as you need it. Its sweet spicy flavour is good for pulse-based soups, with chicken or eggs and in hot drinks.

Paprika (*Paprika/Pimientón*)

Paprika is the powder of finely ground, dried sweet peppers. It can vary considerably in strength. Use in stews and with chicken.

Pepper (*Pimienta*)

No explanation is required here. Pepper can be bought ground or whole. There really is no substitute for freshly milled pepper.

Saffron (*Azafrán*)

Weight for weight, saffron is the most expensive substance in the world. When you consider that 70-80,000 of the crocus-like flowers are needed to produce just 1 lb of saffron, it really isn't surprising. Valencian saffron is considered to be the finest in the world. Saffron should be fresh and bright orange in colour, with a sweet, pungent smell. It can be purchased powdered or, preferably, in little dried filaments. One filament, soaked in warm water or stock and then added, strained or unstrained, to the recipe is enough to colour and flavour 1 lb of rice. Turmeric is sometimes used as a substitute and, although its colouring properties are similar, it does not have the same flavour or character.

SUNDRIES

Bread (*Pan*)

Bread is an essential accompaniment to every Spanish meal. The most popular bread is much shorter and thicker than a French loaf and has a chewy crust and a fairly crumbly texture. Spanish bread should be eaten as fresh as possible. Day-old bread will dry out very quickly.

Sliced bread, buns and rolls, both brown and white, can be bought in the supermarkets. You may find that the sliced bread is not quite as dense as ours but it is excellent for toasting. Wholemeal bread (*pan integrál*) and slimmer's bread (*pan dieta*) are also on sale.

Do as the Spanish do and use your bread to mop up sauces and dressings. Nobody will look askance.

Butter (*Mantequilla*)

The Spanish diet does not rely on butter, which is just as well since it is rather an expensive commodity. Olive oil has always been employed where we would normally use butter. The Spanish even spread olive oil on their bread! Nonetheless, both imported butter and Spanish butter are available and are, in the main, very good. Salted butter is usually wrapped in gold foil paper and labelled *con sal* or *salada*. Unsalted butter, generally more popular, is wrapped in silver foil and, in the case of imported unsalted butter, will be labelled with the words *sin sal*. Butter can also be bought in unwrapped 'slab' form from most of the large covered markets.

It is well worth trying to get used to cooking with oil rather than butter, as the distinctive flavour of olive oil is essential if you wish to create a truly authentic Spanish flavour for your recipes. If you do use butter for frying, add a little olive oil. This will help to prevent the butter from burning.

Cheese (*Queso*)

Spain is not recognised as a great cheese-producing country. You will not find such a rich variety of cheeses as you can buy in France, but there is still a wide choice of good-quality cheeses available. It is only in the north of Spain that lush pasturelands can support the grazing of large numbers of dairy cows. In the drier central and southern regions it is more commonly sheep or goat's milk which is the base ingredient.

Imported cheeses, famous cheeses such as Camembert and Brie (which are made under licence in Spain) and processed cheese are all easily obtainable. Processed cheese is sliced in vacuum-packs or packed in wedges in round cardboard cartons. Most supermarkets will offer a selection, but the market is the best place to purchase fresh cheese. It is here that you will see displays of true Spanish cheeses. Trial and error is the only way to establish which cheese you like, but the following guidelines should help to remove some of the element of hit and miss.

Alicante This cheese is made from goat's milk but has a surprisingly mild, smooth flavour.

Burgos Always eaten young, *burgos* has a soft, almost creamy consistency and can be enjoyed with fruit and honey.

Cabrales Predominantly made from cow's milk with a little ewe and goat's milk added. It is a matured, semi-hard cheese, cylindrical in shape. It has a darkish-grey rind onto which maple leaves are pressed to help retain the flavour. The curd is yellowish-white and has blue/green veins. It has a strong, slightly piquant flavour.

Gallego A mild, yellow curd cheese made from cow's milk. It has a pale yellow rind and a flattened, round shape.

Grazelma This cheese is available well-matured or semi-matured. It is made from ewe's mik and the curd is pale in colour with an excellent flavour. The semi-cured *grazelma* has a milder taste.

Mahón One of Spain's better-known cheeses, *mahón* cheese is made only on the island of Menorca. It has a pale yellow, fatty rind and the cheese is dense, yellowish-white, with tiny pinprick holes. Made from cow's milk, this cheese has a highly individual flavour and aroma. If you prefer your cheese on the mild side, look for younger *mahón* cheese. It is usually sold well-matured and semi-matured.

Perilla A firm cheese with rather a bland flavour, somewhat similar to a mild Cheddar. It is made from cow's milk.

Roncál This cheese is one of the most popular in Spain. It is cylindrical in shape with a hard, thick rind. The rind can be straw-coloured or brown and occasionally it is dotted with mould. The cheese itself is hard and close-grained with a few small holes. It is light yellow, with a good, full, rather piquant flavour.

Requesón A light, curd cheese with a delicious mild flavour.

San Simón This is excellent for those who enjoy a smoked cheese. It is shaped rather like a pear and has an amber-coloured, shiny rind.

Manchego True *manchego* cheese is made exclusively from ewe's milk and is Spain's most popular cheese. It is cylindrical, with a hard, straw-coloured rind. Mature *manchego* has a strong flavour and is dry and fairly hard. The younger cheeses are milder, with a creamy consistency. There are a number of other types of *manchego* cheese, usually made with cow's milk. This type has a greenish/black rind.

Villalón An ideal cheese for those who like a mild flavour and a good choice for slimmers. It is shaped like a small loaf and is sold salted (*con sal*) or unsalted (*sin sal*).

Eggs (*Huevos*)

Eggs play an important part in the Spanish diet. They are usually sold packed in 6-egg cartons, and there are three grades available. In the markets you can often buy eggs ungraded and loose. The price of eggs is much the same as here, although market prices are usually cheaper.

Flour (*Harina*)

You won't be able to buy self-raising flour. Spanish cooks use baking powder (*levadura en polvo*) as a raising agent. Plain flour (*harina de trigo*) and wholemeal flour (*harina integral*) are sold in bags.

Margarine (*Margarina*)

You will recognise some of the brands of margarine. It is sold in tubs or in blocks. As you would expect, it is considerably cheaper than butter.

Milk (*Leche*)

Both pasteurised and long-life (UHT) milk is sold in Spain as well as skimmed (*desnatada*) and sterilised (*esterilizada*). For cooking purposes it is worth looking out for powdered milk (*leche en polvo*). It is sold in tins and in bags. Pasteurised milk is sold in litre cartons and is date-stamped, so you can check for freshness. The taste is similar to our milk but some sensitive tea-drinkers find its slightly 'cooked' flavour unpleasant.

Oil (*Aceite*)

The olive is the most common tree in Spain and, with a staggering 425,000 metric tons of olive oil (*aceite de oliva*), produced every year, it is hardly surprising that olive oil, for both cooking and dressing, is the first choice for Spanish housewives and an essential ingredient in most traditional Spanish recipes. Olive oil has a unique flavour and is an excellent cooking medium. It does not decompose easily when frying at high temperatures. It is, without doubt, the best oil for dressing salads.

Most olive oil is refined to reduce the acid flavour of virgin oil. But you will see three types on sale in Spain: virgin oil, unrefined, with the highest acidity and the most robust flavour; refined olive oil, the most subtle in flavour; and pure olive oil, a blend of virgin and refined.

If you prefer a lighter oil you can buy sunflower oil (*aceite de gírasol*), corn oil (*germen de maiz*) or peanut oil (*aceite de cacahuetes*).

Olives (*Olivas*)

Don't be tempted to pick olives and eat them straight from the tree. It will be a horrible experience for your palate. They are extremely bitter and it is only after they have been processed that they are edible. There are many different varieties of olives. Some are reserved solely for the making of olive oil, while others are set aside for eating. Spanish olives are very good and you will be able to find quite a wide selection bottled in brine in supermarkets. The best way, without a doubt, to buy olives is from the municipal markets. Here, usually in the fruit and vegetable sections, there is almost always a stall specialising in olives and other pickled fruit and vegetables. You will see huge, plump black and green olives and olives containing a wide variety of stuffings. Red pepper is one of the most common, but look out for olives stuffed with almonds and anchovies.

Olives are an acquired taste. If you don't enjoy eating them on their own you may enjoy their taste when mixed with other ingredients in recipes such as stuffed tomatoes. If you do enjoy them, you are in for a real treat. The price of olives in Spain, particularly in the markets, is well below the average price here.

Pasta (*Pasta*)

The Spanish use pasta a great deal, especially in soups. Both tinned pasta dishes and packets of dried pasta can be purchased all over Spain.

Pastries (*Pasteles*), Cakes (*Bollos*) and Biscuits (*Galletas*)

If you are on a diet, steer well clear of Spanish bakeries. The average Spaniard has an excessively sweet tooth, and, although pastries and cakes are rarely eaten as a 'sweet' course, they are consumed for breakfast, for 'elevenses', for mid-afternoon snacks and late at night.

You will find that most of the cakes and pastries are sweeter than those baked here but the quality is excellent. Meringues, custards, eclairs and 'Danish' are all good.

Many of the cakes and biscuits use almonds and honey as a base ingredient. Try *mantecadas*, an Andalucian speciality, but available throughout Spain. It has a crumbly texture, somewhat similar to shortbread but much lighter. Sweet breads such as *suizos* (sugar-coated rolls) are popular both for breakfast and at teatime and doughnuts rank with the best available here.

Preserves (*Confitura/Mermelada*)

Mermelada means any form of jam. If you want marmalade, look for *mermelada de naranja*. And, if you like your marmalade very bitter, look for jars labelled *mermelada de naranja amarga*. There is a wide selection of jams on sale and in the main the jars will have a picture of the fruit ingredient on the label. Honey (*miel*) is of excellent quality and a wide range of exotic honeys can be bought in healthfood shops.

Pulses

Pulses are the dried seeds of such plants as peas, lentils and soya, haricot and butter beans. They are widely used throughout Spain but particularly in the north and the islands.

Chick-peas (Garbanzos)
Chick-peas feature in many Spanish dishes and have a unique flavour reminiscent of chestnuts.

Basic Preparation Soak for 24 hours. Place in a heavy pan and cover with water. Season well and add a sliced onion and a crushed garlic clove. Bring to the boil and then simmer gently for approximately 6 hours in a slow oven.

Lentils (Lentejas)
Lentils are a valuable source of protein and play an important part in the Spanish diet. There are a number of varieties, but those from the Canary Islands have the best flavour. They can be red, green or greenish-brown. Lentils should be thoroughly washed and checked for stones and grit. They can be used in soups and stews or cold in salads.

Basic Preparation Cover the lentils with cold water and bring to the boil. Remove from the heat and allow to stand for 1 hour. Add seasoning and a chopped onion and bring back to the boil. Simmer for 10-15 minutes or until tender.

Red Beans/White Beans (Habichuela Rojo/Habichuela Blanco)

Red and white beans are often served on their own or as a vegetable accompaniment. They are also included in soups and stews. These beans should be washed and soaked for at least 12 hours in cold water.

Basic Preparation Place the soaked beans in a large pan and cover with water. Bring to the boil over a high heat. Cover the pan, lower the heat and simmer for approximately 40 minutes. Drain and serve hot with butter or a sauce. Or they can be left to cool and then added to salads.

Rice (*Arróz*)

Valencia is the most important rice-growing region in Spain and the short, stubby rice-grain cultivated here is the basis of Spain's famous national dish — *paella*. Throughout Spain, rice is a staple food and you will see it included in many restaurant dishes. There are three main types available: short-grain (*arróz a la Valenciana*); long-grain (*arróz*); and brown rice (*arróz integrál*).

HERBS, SPICES, SUNDRIES AND STAPLES

Vocabulary

Basil	*Albahaca*
Bay	*Laurel*
Coriander	*Culantro*
Chives	*Cebollinas*
Dill	*Eneldo*
Fennel	*Hinojo*
Garlic	*Ajo*
Herbs	*Hierbas*
Marjoram	*Mejorana*
Mint	*Menta*
Parsley	*Perejíl*
Rosemary	*Romero*
Sage	*Salvia*
Tarragon	*Estragón*
Thyme	*Tomillo*
Chilli	*Chili*
Cinnamon	*Canela*
Cloves	*Clavos*

Cumin	*Comino*
Nutmeg	*Nuez Moscada*
Paprika	*Páprika/Pimientón*
Pepper	*Pimienta*
Saffron	*Azafrán*
Spices	*Especias*
Almonds	*Almendras*
Baking Powder	*Levadura en Polvo*
Beans	*Habichuelas*
Biscuits	*Galletas*
Brazil Nuts	*Castañas de Brazil*
Bread	*Pan*
Butter	*Mantequilla*
Cakes	*Bollos*
Cashew Nuts	*Anacardos*
Cheese	*Queso*
Chick-peas	*Garbanzos*
Chocolate	*Chocolate*
Milk Chocolate	*Chocolate con leche*
Plain Chocolate	*Chocolate solo*
Corn Oil	*Germen de Maiz*
Cream	*Nata*
Crisps	*Patatas Fritas*
Doughnuts	*Donut*
Eggs	*Huevos*
Flour	*Harina*
Hamburgers	*Hamburguesas*
Hazelnuts	*Avellanas*
Honey	*Miel*
Ice-cream	*Helado*
Preserves	*Confitura/Mermelada*
Lentils	*Lentejas*
Margarine	*Margarina*
Milk	*Leche*
Mustard	*Mostaza*
Nuts	*Nueces*
Oil	*Aceite*
Olive Oil	*Aceite de Oliva*
Olives	*Olivas*
Pasta	*Pasta*
Pastries	*Pasteles*
Peanuts	*Cacahuetes*
Peanut Oil	*Aceite de Cacahuetes*
Rice	*Arróz*
Salt	*Sal*

Sandwiches	*Bocadillos*
Sugar	*Azucár*
Tea	*Té*

Phrases

How much is this?	*Cuánto cuesta esto?*
Please write it down	*Escríbamelo por favor*
Do you have any ...?	*Tiene usted ...?*
I'd like ...	*Quisiera*
I'd like that	*Quisiera ese*
What is this?	*Qué es esto?*
I would like ... kilo(s) of	*Quisiera ... kilo(s) de ...*

7

WINES, SPIRITS AND BEVERAGES

If a thing is worth doing, it's worth doing to excess. And Spain is a wonderful place for doing it — not only because of the minimal outlay necessary to maintain non-stop euphoria, but also because of the great variety of good wines and spirits with which to do so.

Spanish wine is dismissed by many wine snobs as unworthy of consideration. Indeed there are some ghastly wines to be found in Spain — wines that bypass the usual qualities of delicate bouquet, pleasant taste, through merriment and elation — and plunge you straight into a vinegary black stupor with a thick head and deep depression. Heaven preserve us from such wines. But, with a minimum of effort and armed with this book, you should be able to avoid the pitfalls and make the most of drinking in Spain.

The vine has been cultivated for nearly 2000 years here. The Romans apparently introduced it, and so successful was their viticulture that a constant procession of ships sailed up the Tiber to Rome laden with amphorae of Spanish wine. The Moors, rampaging up from Africa in 711 AD, put a stop to the development of the wine industry, although it is certain that many of these Moslems were discreet tipplers. With the completion of the Christian reconquest in 1492, the Spaniards returned enthusiastically to the cultivation and drinking of wine.

In 1850-60, as the phylloxera disease ravaged the vines of France, a number of leading French wine-growers arrived south of the Cantabrian mountains, in the plain of the Rio Oja. Here they found climate and conditions similar to that of their native Bordeaux. Several settled here and brought their more advanced French methods to Spanish wine-making. Partly as a result of this influence, Rioja is the most notable wine in Spain today.

Rioja

The Rioja district is in north-central Spain, a long run if you're holidaying on the coast, and not recommended in the heat of summer. Rioja wines are available all over the country, and are looked upon as something of a luxury at 200-300 pesetas a bottle. It doesn't matter where you are, you can buy Rioja in every supermarket, wine-shop and bar.

I would say even a bad Rioja is good — but I would be laying myself wide open, for I've never had a bad one. Rioja is particularly distinctive for its 'oaky' flavour. This is a legacy of the Frenchmen who arrived in the nineteenth century. Previously, wine had been made in vast, open tubs, with grapes, stalks and leaves all being tossed into the brew. The French suggested that the rubbish be left out, and the wine be matured in oak casks, as was then the custom in France. Today, most Rioja is matured in casks of American oak, which imparts a wonderful woody flavour (oak contains vanillin, which gives it a hint of vanilla).

Check out your bottle of Rioja by looking at the label on the back. It should have a stamp with 'Rioja' written diagonally across it, and '*Denominacion de Origén*' round the edge. You will also find a map of the Rioja district with its three different regions — Rioja Alta, Rioja Alavesa, and Rioja Baja. The best is the Alta, in the west, near the Atlantic. In the east, the Baja area, the Mediterranean climate has a greater influence, producing poorer-quality wines.

Other legends to look out for are: *vino sin crianza* — inexpensive table wine, sold off any time with no ageing; *vino de crianza*, which must have been aged in oak casks and be sold not less than three years after harvest to qualify for this label; and *reserva*, which has to age for a minimum of two years in the wood and one in the bottle. The *gran reserva* is only selected from exceptional harvests. It must spend three years in the wood, two in the bottle, and may not be sold until seven years after harvesting.

The vintage (*vendimia*) or year of harvest (*cosecha*) is also on the label. Rioja, through skilful blending, is of consistently good quality, but 1971 and 1977 were wretched years, washed out by rain and rot; 1964, 1970 and 1978 were exceptional years. Other years are just good. Take the cork out a few hours before drinking, as with all reds, and away you go. Highly recommended are the Marques de Riscal, Carta de Plata, and Carta de Oro.

Penedés

On the Barcelona coast you're in wine-growing country. The

Penedés area starts around Sitges and sprawls up the mountains inland. Traditionally an area known for its inexpensive table wine, this *denominacion de origén*, or wine region, has recently undergone a radical shake-up. Today the wines of Penedés are beginning to rival those of Rioja as the fine wines of Spain. Torres is the biggest *bodega* in the region, and these wines are carrying off prize after prize at exhibitions. You could do worse than the red *Tres Torres* (Sangre de Toro), or the delicious, dry white, *viña sol*, huge quantities of which are exported. There are also many other small *bodegas* worth trying.

Alella

Twenty miles north of Barcelona, on the coast, is the tiny wine-growing patch of Alella, with less than 1,000 acres of vines and only two *bodegas*. The name to go for here is Marfil, available in red, white or rosé. It's not exported and doesn't even travel around Spain much, so you can only enjoy it here. These wines are usually bottled and sold young — fruity and delicious.

Lo Corriente

Although Rioja is the best-known and perhaps the most important wine region in Spain, its output, at a mere 120 million litres a year, is only a tiny fraction of Spain's total wine production. The bulk comes from the central areas of La Mancha and Valdepeñas, the baking hot, dry table-lands where Don Quixote tilted at windmills. Here, highly productive grapes are drenched in a constant blaze of sunshine, month after month. The result is an immense harvest of coarse red wine — very high in alcohol, but low in quality. Some 40 per cent of this goes to make industrial alcohol; the other 60 per cent is drunk raw and raunchy all over Spain, or doctored and made unrecognisable by the big wine-blending factories. But even here, the more enlightened wine-producers are at work upgrading the quality of their wines. In five or ten years' time, the wines of this region may well achieve a very acceptable international quality. No wonder the French and Italians are so concerned about Spain's admission to the EEC.

Sparkling Wines

Spanish sparkling wines, too, are being improved. Again the hardened wine-man will look down his delicate nose at Spanish champagne. But Cordorníu, Freixenet and Castellblanch produce very high-quality wines by the *méthode*

Champenoise. These vast, modern *bodegas* are to be found in the hideous town of San Sadurni de Noya, an hour's drive south-west from Barcelona. You can visit these *bodegas*, and it's well worth the trip to see the astonishing process of making these sparkling wines. The label to look for is 'Cava', as sparkling wines made by the *méthode Champenoise* are called. The driest is 'Brut Natur', then 'Brut', 'Seco', 'Semi-seco', 'Semi-dulce', and, sweetest of all, 'Dulce'. These wines are serious rivals to many French champagnes, although they are not permitted to use the name 'Champagne'.

There are two other methods by which sparkling wine is made. The least objectionable of the two is *cuve close*, where the secondary fermentation is carried out in big tanks. But steer clear of *gasificado*, a vile brew made by pumping carbon dioxide into poor-quality white wines. A popular habit among Spaniards is to add *limonada* (lemonade) to red wine to make a long, sweet, highly alcoholic drink. Try it, it's really very good. Cava is bottled in normal-sized champagne bottles, also in magnums. A little bigger is the *jeroboam*; more enormous still is a *matusalem*; and finally there is the immense *salamanzar*.

Vega Sicilia

The queen of Spanish wines is known as 'Vega Sicilia'. It's very rare, difficult to find and costs the earth. It grows in a tiny wine-growing area near Valladolid, and, in the unlikely event that you get an opportunity to try it, do — you won't find anything else like it in Spain. There are two types, both red — 'Valbuena' and 'Reserva Unico'.

Málaga

Southern Spain does not grow table wines. The soil is chalk, with a little clay and sand, mercilessly baked by the sun ten months of the year. The vines need to be drought-resistant, hard and tough, but they are no good for ordinary wine. Malaga has been a wine-producing area since Roman times. It produces a thick, sweet *vino negro* or black wine, using the Moscatel grape. If you like sweet wine, this is very good indeed, especially to end a meal. Just ask for 'Malaga'.

Xeres/Jerez (Sherry)

Further west is the world's most remarkable wine-growing area. Centred around Jerez de la Frontera is the sherry-producing region, a tiny patch based on three towns — Jerez, Sanlucar de Barrameda and Puerto de Santa Maria. If the wine has not lain in casks in one of these three towns, it is not a sherry. Here the vines are really 'hard'; the grape used is called *palomino*. Our word for sherry comes, perhaps, from a corruption of the word 'Jerez', or perhaps from the Persian 'Shariz', where sweet wines were grown. In Shakespeare's time it was already drunk in England, and known as Sack. The big *bodegas* and shippers are household names throughout the world: Domecq (originally from France), Gonzalez Byass (Byass was a Welshman), Harveys of Bristol, to name just a few.

Sherry is the most popular drink in Spain — hundreds of thousands of litres of sherry are brewed specially for the *ferias* held in places such as Jerez and Seville. I like it best cold, in a glass crammed with ice. A bottle of dry *fino* should be consumed within a couple of days of opening, as it quickly loses it fresh dryness. Or, better still, wolf the lot at one sitting.

There are many different types of sherry. *Fino* is the driest; La Ina and Tio Pepe are good examples — pale and dry, and great for an aperitif. *Manzanilla* is a *fino* matured in Sanlucar de Barrameda, where the Atlantic breezes whipping across the estuary of the Guadalquivir — great river of the Moors — are said to impart a salty tang to the wine. *Amontillado* is a deeper amber colour, a bit nutty, and fairly heavily fortified by the addition of grape spirit. *Oloroso* is dark, soft, full-bodied and rather sweeter — real nectar. Cream sherry, developed for the British and American markets, is sweetened and thickened by skilful blending.

Sherry too is aged for years in oak casks, the young and old wines being slowly blended together to give a consistently high quality. There is no vintage year on a bottle of sherry, for each harvest is added to the same casks. Old sherry-barrels are much in demand for making malt whisky, for it is from the sherry-soaked wood that the pale gold of the whisky comes. Brandy uses the same process.

The best places to sample sherries and wines are the *bodegas* — great cool stone rooms lined with tiers of huge barrels. The floor is covered with sawdust and olive pips. The drink is anything you like, blended or straight, fresh from the tap sunk into the barrel. This is, to me, the best way to drink wines and sherries — take a bucket to fill up for home consumption.

Montilla

Further inland, nearer Córdoba, lies the Montilla region. Here the soil characteristics are similar to those at Jerez, and the area is justifiably known as *el Sartén*, the frying-pan of

Spain, because of the intense heat. Here the grape used is the Pedro Ximenez, a fat rich grape bursting with sugars. The wines of Montilla, which are now enjoying a greater popularity than ever, are naturally fortified — nothing is added or taken away. They tend to be sweeter than the sherries and less alcoholic, but quite as delicious.

Spirits

If you don't have money to burn, keep off the Scotch. Obviously it is all imported and costs the earth. The same with French cognac, but Spanish *coñac* is very good — sweeter than the French and very much cheaper. Spanish *coñac* is made in much the same way as sherry: the distilled wine, having first been reduced to about 40 per cent alcohol, and mixed with a little treacle for sweetness and caramelised sugar for colour, is matured in old sherry-soaked wooden barrels, the younger spirit gradually being mixed with the more mature in the barrels below. This is called the *solera* method. The cheaper brandies are rough and warming, particularly good in coffee. But as you go up the price-scale you will find delicious 'rounded' spirits.

Brandy is really Spain's national drink — 25 million bottles are made in Jerez alone every year. It is taken first thing every morning, before the farmer goes to his fields, or the factory worker to his bench, as a warmer with a strong cup of coffee. It is taken mid-morning with anything you fancy. No meal is complete without a glass of *coñac*. There's Osborne, Fundador, Carlos 1, 103, Magno, Torres, Soberano — too many to mention. Order it by brand name.

Gin is cheap and made in Spain, though the imported varieties are more expensive than at home. Order the brand name — so *gin larios* brings you a cheap gin from Málaga, while *gin Gordon* is the more expensive British brand. Gin and tonic is simply *Gintónica*. Vodka is also imported and not particularly cheap.

Every bar has a huge selection of liqueurs, many made from the most bizarre ingredients. Try Artichoke liqueur, banana, mango or one of the dozens of herb liqueurs made from secret recipes dating back hundreds of years. The Spanish favourite is *anís* or *pastís* — a strong aniseed drink like Ricard in France and Ouzo in Greece — refreshing with ice and water.

Beer

It is not easy to enthuse over Spanish beer, but it fills the gap and, apart from the odd bar selling Guinness and German and Dutch lager (made under licence in Spain) it's all there is. Spanish beers Estrella Dorada, San Miguél, El Aguila, etc. are all much the same and not altogether disagreeable. But they don't quench your thirst, and they blow you up with gas ... Just ask for *cerveza* — *un caña de cerveza* is a bigger glass. Beer mostly comes *en botella* — bottled — but it is also available from the barrel (*de barríl*) or on draught (*presión*). A *cervecería* is a bar where they specialise in beer, but the only variation I have found on the basic fare is *cerveza negra* — a thick black beer with a licorice taste, like stout.

Sangria

Sangria — a great Spanish invention — is much better for quenching your thirst. You can make it with sweet Spanish brandy, one of the cheap red wines, fruit juice, soda-water and fruit. Change the quantities to suit your mood and the time of day. You can also buy bottles of ready-made Sangria — a pointless exercise since it takes away all the pleasure of fooling around with the mixing of the drink (see recipe section).

Fruit Juices

'Natural' fruit juices are plentiful in Spain, but are generally not quite as natural as they could be. Sometimes you can get freshly squeezed orange-juice, but not often, and it is surprisingly dear. The juice sold in bottles and tins is often artificially sweetened, flavoured and coloured.

Horchata

In the Balearic Islands and on the Valencia coast you will be fortunate enough to enjoy fresh, natural *horchata*. Drunk with a straw from a tall glass clinking with ice, this is one of the most delicious drinks I know. It is made from 'tiger-nuts' (a type of groundnut) and milk, sweetened with honey, and I'm not sure the occasional ground almond doesn't find its way in too. It sounds disgusting, but it isn't, and it's non-alcoholic. Nowadays you can get good *horchata* all over Spain, but the canned and bottled varieties are feeble imitations.

Coffee

Spanish coffee is glorious, made in espresso machines with freshly ground beans — strong and slightly bitter. When ordering, *café* secures a tiny cup or glass of rich, inky brown coffee; *café doble* gets you a double ration; and *doble con leche* makes a good breakfast sopped up with a 'donut'. If you don't like strong coffee, or if it disagrees with you, you can always buy *descafeinado* or powdered Nescafe. This can be bought in any supermarket and ordered in any bar, but it tends to be more expensive than at home.

Tea

Tea is a bit of a dead loss in Spain — all you get is a cup of hot water and a bag. In the tourist resorts they have come round to putting the bags in a pot, but not much skill and care goes into the making of tea, and the determined tea-drinker remains to the Spaniard an amusing curiosity.

Water

Bottled water abounds: still (*sin gaz*) and bubbly (*con gaz*). You can drink tap-water pretty well everywhere in Spain, but bottled water is cheap and generally tastes much better.

WINES, SPIRITS AND BEVERAGES

Vocabulary

Bottle	*Botella*
Carafe	*Garrafa*
Glass	*Vaso*
Half-bottle	*Media botella*
Litre	*Litro*
Dry	*Seco*
Sparkling	*Espumoso*
Sweet	*Dulce*

Alcoholic Drinks

Red	*Tinto*
White	*Blanco*
Rosé	*Rosé*
Beer	*Cerveza*
Brandy	*Coñac*
Gin	*Gin*
Gin and tonic	*Gintónica*
Liqueur	*Licor*
Port	*Vino de Oporto*
Rum	*Ron*
Rum and coke	*Cuba libre*
Whisky	*Whisky*
Whisky and soda	*Whisky con soda*
Sherry	*Jerez*
Vodka	*Vodka*

Vermouth	*Vermouth*
Wine	*Vino*

Beverages

Coffee	*Café*
Coffee with milk	*Café con leche*
Black coffee	*Café solo*
Expresso	*Café exprés*
Tea	*Té*
Tea with milk	*Té con leche*
Tea with lemon	*Té con limón*
Iced tea	*Té helado*
Hot chocolate	*Chocolate caliente*

Cold Drinks

Fruit juice	*Jugo de fruta*
Lemonade	*Limonada*
Orangeade	*Naranjada*
Milkshake	*Batido*
Mineral water	*Agua mineral*

8

SHOPPING
IN SPAIN

One of the problems of shopping abroad is unfamiliarity. We become so used to the layouts of supermarkets and our local grocery stores, so familiar with the colours, shapes and sizes of the brands we buy regularly, that shopping in a foreign country can be a very disorientating experience. At home, as often as not, you will make a beeline for what you need and zip round the supermarket quickly and efficiently. Abroad, unfamiliar arrangements of products and different labelling and grading can be rather difficult at first. So, take your time, be prepared to make the occasional mistake and enjoy the enormous variety available.

Almost all Spanish coastal resorts and major towns have well-stocked hypermarkets, often located just outside the town and with their own parking facilities. These stores carry everything you would expect to find at home, and often a great deal more. Certainly, they are excellent for stocking up a basic larder at the beginning of your stay, and the prices, as at home, are often more reasonable than at smaller shops in the towns.

Hypermarkets and supermarkets carry all the usual groceries, dry goods and frozen foods and some have substantial meat and vegetable sections, as well as good dairy departments and delicatessen counters selling cold, sliced meats, Spanish sausages and ready-made salads. They will often sell barbecue fuel, garden furniture, picnic goods, kitchen utensils and toilet requisites as well.

You will recognise quite a few brand names in the supermarkets and, although some of these products are imported (and this will be reflected in the price), most of the familiar names will be made under licence in Spain and will differ slightly in taste from their counterparts at home.

The range of alcoholic beverages available in these shops

is very comprehensive. You will recognise many of the brands, but not the prices. Generally speaking, hypermarkets and larger supermarkets are the best places, pricewise, to stock up your drinks cupboard and often present far better value for money than the duty-free shops at airports (see chapter on Wines, Spirits and Liqueurs).

All major towns have their own butchers' shops (*carnicería*), fishmongers (*pescadería*), seafood shops (*marisccería*) and greengrocers (*verdulero*). There are two types of bakers' shops: *panaderías*, selling ordinary bread; and *pastelerías*, which sell sweet breads and cakes. Market shopping is generally the most popular with Spanish housewives and is always easier on the purse, and a great deal more fun, than shopping in supermarkets.

Most major towns and coastal resorts have a *mercado municipál*, usually divided into three sections: meat, fruit and vegetables and fish. You will be impressed by the cleanliness of these markets and the wide variety of produce available. They are always very well patronised, particularly early in the morning when the canny Spanish housewife is always there to buy the pick of the crop. The noise in these markets is deafening. Stallholders yell at each other in rapid Spanish above the din of chattering housewives who discuss and examine the produce minutely before they buy.

Forget about queuing. It is a complete waste of time and will leave you with a strong feeling of injustice. You must jostle for position, keeping your eye firmly fixed on the stall-holder. You will be served eventually. Indeed, if there is a substantial crowd around a particular stall it will invariably mean that the produce is especially good or that it is on offer at a special price. These markets are open daily except Sundays. Check with your tourist office for any local variations. The earlier you go, the better the selection.

Many Spanish towns have a once-weekly open market. Again, check with the tourist office to find which is market day in your area. It is here that the farmers and craftsmen from the surrounding area come to sell their wares. The prices are generally much cheaper than in the supermarkets and often beat the prices in the *mercado municipales*. You can haggle in this type of market, but only over craft items such as leather, jewellery, ceramics and basketware. Again, it pays to get to these markets as early as possible.

One point worth remembering when shopping either in the smaller, town-based shops or markets is that transactions are always for cash and the acceptance of credit cards is very rare.

If your apartment or villa is not equipped with everything you need in the way of general household tools or cleaning equipment, you will be able to buy anything you need from the hypermarket or from a *droguería* which sells not medicines, as the name implies, but soap powders, mops, brooms and general cleaning materials. Ironmongers are called *ferreterías* and carry the normal selection of hardware items you would expect to find. *Farmacías* are chemist shops, often selling cosmetics and perfumes as well, but *perfumerías* sell only perfumes and cosmetics, not medication. Stamps can be purchased at a post office (*correos*) or at tobacconists (*tabacalería*). Incidentally, cigarettes are much cheaper than here with some of the inexpensive Spanish brands costing less than half the price and working out even cheaper than duty-free tobacco.

With regard to opening times, Spanish shops usually open between 8.30 and 9.00 am, close for lunch at around 1.00 and re-open again at 4.30 till around 8.30 pm. In some tourist areas the shops stay open even later and may even open on Sundays. Bakers and supermarkets will often open on a Sunday morning but you cannot rely on this. In major cities such as Barcelona, Málaga and Seville the department stores stay open all afternoon and this is often the best time to shop as they are much less crowded.

The word *rebajas* in a shop window indicates a sale is in progress. Unfortunately, these signs have become a permanent fixture in the windows of many shops in the tourist resorts. Their owners, one presumes, are working on the premise that most tourists only stay for a short period of time and they would not know the sign had been there all year. Of course, there are genuine sales but it really does pay to look around before buying and compare prices. A trip to the nearest major city to shop where the natives shop will really pay dividends. It is simply not done to haggle in Spanish shops. Leave the bargaining to the open markets.

If your mental arithmetic is not as agile as it should be, it can be very useful to carry your own reckoner with you, written on a small piece of paper. Unfortunately, exchange rates are not designed for convenience, but if you reckon on allowing 200 pesetas to the £1 sterling or 160 pesetas to the dollar, it will help you to calculate quickly how much you are being asked to pay in roughly equivalent terms. If you ask the price of anything in Spanish and the answer is too rapid to understand, ask the shopkeeper to write the figure down. They are quite used to this, but it will help if you keep a small notepad and pencil handy.

One final point to bear in mind. Spanish housewives are fussy shoppers and, particularly when it comes to food, expect and get the highest quality. Shop assistants and stall-holders are, for the most part, much more prepared to go to a great deal of trouble mincing, cleaning, cutting, chopping and preparing your purchases to almost any specification even when you are buying fairly small quantities. This can be extremely irritating, as it causes long delays while you are waiting to be served. But remember, with an attempt at the language, you will be extended the same quality of service when it comes to your turn.

SHOPPING IN SPAIN

Vocabulary

Bakers	*Panadería*
	Pastelería
Bank	*Banco*
Bookshop	*Librería*
Butchers	*Carnicería*
Chemist	*Farmacía*
Fishmongers	*Pescadería*
Greengrocers	*Verdulería*
Ironmonger	*Ferretería*
Market	*Mercado*
Post Office	*Correos*
Tobacconist	*Tabacalería*
Sale	*Rebaja*
Seafood Shop	*Mariscería*
Supermarket	*Supermercado*

Phrases

How much is this?	*Cuanto cuesta esto?*
Please write it down	*Escríbamelo por favor*
Do you have any …?	*Tiene usted …?*
I would like a …	*Quisiera un …*
I'd like that	*Quisiera ese*
What is this?	*Que es esto?*
Can you show me …?	*Puede usted enseñarme …?*
I'll take it	*Me lo llevo*
Can I pay by travellers' cheque?	*Puedo pagar con cheque de viajero?*
Do you take credit cards?	*Accepta usted tarjetas de crédito?*

9

WHAT TO TAKE WITH YOU

The equipping of kitchens in self-catering apartments or villas varies considerably, but it is quite unlikely that you will be provided with everything you need for ambitious cookery. This is not to suggest that you should give up valuable suitcase space for kitchen utensils, or that you should board your flight festooned with pots and pans, but there are a few gadgets which will make life easier and preparation less time-consuming.

Corkscrew

There is almost bound to be a corkscrew provided. But if you have a good one that you are used to it may well pay to take it with you. It will be put to good and constant use.

Electric Blender

This is possibly the most useful gadget of all and can save a great deal of time and effort. It will help you to produce delicious soups and sauces quickly and efficiently, in particular *gazpacho* which can be made in a matter of minutes with a blender. It can also be used for stuffings, for iced coffee, milk-shakes and puréeing fruit and vegetables.

Garlic Press

Garlic is widely used in Spanish cooking. A good-quality garlic press won't take up much room in your luggage and you will be very glad to have it.

Knives

Any good kitchen should be equipped with sharp knives. Spanish cooking involves a great deal of vegetable chopping, and a good, sharp knife is invaluable. If you take your favourite knife with you, make sure the blade is well wrapped and don't carry it in your hand baggage. It could result in some embarrassing moments at airport checks.

Measures

The Spanish use the metric system. Take with you a set of plastic metric kitchen measures and a small, plastic liquid measuring jug. This will make cooking a great deal easier and is better than making rough guesses.

Travel Plug

It will save a lot of time and temper if you buy a travel plug before you go instead of changing all the plugs on any electrical items you take with you. In most parts of Spain the voltage is 110-125 volts, but occasionally you will come across 220-230 volts.

Anything else you may need should already be provided but be prepared to improvise. It might be useful to take a thermos flask with you for picnics or long days spent on the beach, and, if you plan to barbecue, a set of skewers would be helpful.

Sometimes the ovens fitted in holiday apartments have minds of their own and if you plan to do any cooking that requires precise temperatures it might be advisable to take an oven thermometer.

Just a quick note about photography. I would suggest you take your films with you and have them developed when you get back. Films and developing and printing are expensive in Spain.

10

BABIES, CHILDREN AND THOSE ON SPECIAL DIETS

SPECIAL DIETS

A high proportion of fresh fish, vegetables and pulses and limited use of animal fats in cooking processes make the Spanish diet one of the healthiest in the world. Visitors to Spain with special dietary requirements should have little problem in adapting the food available to their needs. All the same, it is advisable to check with your doctor before you travel abroad and to make sure that you have all the necessary medical insurance cover.

Health food shops (*tienda dietética*) are to be found in almost all major towns and most carry a comprehensive range of dietary products and vitamin pills, in fact everything you would expect to find in equivalent shops at home. Supermarkets also carry a range of low-calorie or unsweetened products as well as such items as decaffeinated coffee (*cafe descafeinado*) and skimmed milk (*leche desnatada*).

Low-fat Diets

If you are following a low-fat diet, whether for purely health reasons or to lose weight, you will have to be careful when eating out to choose grilled (*asado*) rather than fried (*frito*) food. But, when it comes to shopping and cooking for yourself, this diet should not present a problem. Stick to fish and poultry, sprinkled with lemon juice, herbs and a little water and grilled wrapped in foil parcels. Make good use of the wide selection of vegetables available and prepare salads with a little fish or chopped egg. Keep well away from the bakers' shops and take advantage of the wonderful range of fruit available throughout the year.

Diabetic Diets

You will already be aware of the do's and don'ts of your diabetic regime. Every diabetic has slightly different requirements, often according to the medicinal treatment prescribed. Broadly speaking, balancing your diet carefully and eating regular meals are two important factors and this can be a little difficult when you are on holiday. The Spanish eat lunch and dinner much later than we do although most major resort area restaurants are used to different visitors'mealtimes and it should not be necessary for you to change your eating pattern too drastically. Of course, being on your own allows you complete freedom to plan and take your meals when you wish. You will find a range of diabetic foods in most good health food shops.

High-fibre Diets

A diet which contains a high proportion of cereal and vegetable fibre is a healthy diet for anyone, and following a high-fibre regime will present no problems in Spain. Fresh or dried fruit and nuts and pulses are all easily available and feature in many Spanish recipes.

Wholemeal bread (*pan integrál*) and wholemeal flour (*harina integrál*) are sold in most supermarkets and bakeries. Porridge oats (*copos de avena*) and breakfast cereals are easy to find although All-Bran, or any near equivalent, does not seem to be widely available. If this product is an important part of your diet, you might consider taking it with you.

BABIES

You will have no trouble at all finding baby foods in Spain and the quality will be just as good as here. The Spanish adore their children and a rather disproportionate amount of space is given over to children's products in supermarkets and stores. You will find tinned, puréed baby-foods, powdered milk and rusks and disposable nappies. All these items can be purchased in the larger supermarkets and hypermarkets.

CHILDREN

Providing food for children on holiday can be a nightmare. While you may wish to be adventurous, children are usually less so when it comes to sampling new recipes or foods and will demand dishes which are more familiar. Many of the recipes we have included in this book will appeal to all but the most fussy child. Chicken is usually a favourite and most children enjoy fried fish and omelettes.

If you wish to provide for the children quickly and easily before you turn to cooking more ambitious meals for yourselves, a few convenience foods from the frozen food section of the hypermarket can be a great help. Fishfingers, pizzas, hamburgers and chips, for instance, are all similar to the type we can buy here. You will have no problem identifying these foods as pictures of the product are always clearly shown on the packages. Sardines on toast, cheese on toast, tomato salads are all quick, easy, economical fillers for children. They will certainly enjoy the delicious cakes and pastries and will find the ice-cream (*helado*) of excellent quality. Tubs of ice-cream can be purchased in supermarkets and there is a wide selection of flavours to choose from.

11
EATING AND DRINKING OUT

However much you enjoy catering for yourself, eating out occasionally is a treat, and of course it is good to have someone else to wash the dishes. Eating out is more of a way of life in Spain; often the whole family goes along, virtually taking over a whole restaurant with hordes of relatives, maybe once or twice a week. This is not as extravagant as it sounds, for it is very much cheaper to eat out in Spain than here. It has often seemed to me that it is cheaper to eat at an inexpensive restaurant than to buy the ingredients and do it oneself.

Unfortunately, however, many of the restaurants in the tourist areas serve bland, anonymous food, and many of the bars and restaurants are foreign-owned, and offer nothing even remotely resembling Spanish fare. It seems a pity to travel thousands of miles to eat the same old thing as at home.

Trying to find good restaurants that offer you the opportunity to try real Spanish cooking can be difficult, but a good guide-line — valid wherever you go in the world — is to look out for where the locals themselves eat. If the restaurant is regularly patronised by the Spanish, it is likely to be a good bet.

Many Spanish restaurants are officially graded, with signs showing forks. The number of forks awarded is not necessarily a reflection of the quality of the food, but rather an indication of the luxuriousness of the facilities, and the damage the bill is likely to do your wallet. You will often get an excellent meal in a one-fork or even no-fork establishment, but don't expect the table to be so prettily dressed.

Many restaurants offer a *menú del dia* or a *plato del dia* — a set menu or dish of the day — and these are often very good value, if perhaps not offering the most refined and delicate gastronomy. They will include three courses, bread, and sometimes *vino de la casa* — house wine. You may be lucky to find a set menu featuring a house or local speciality (*especialidad de la casa* or *especialidad des locales*). *Platos combinados* and *menús turisticas* are all set menus along the same lines.

There are a number of other establishments, besides bars and cafés, which do not come under the fork classification, and these are usually found outside the tourist areas. *Ventas* are the nearest Spanish equivalent to transport cafés — rather unsalubrious looking 'dives' by the roadside. But they offer simple, honest food and local wines at rock-bottom prices — very highly recommended.

Fondas, often found in smaller towns or in the old part of larger towns, are basically inns, but in addition to providing cheap, basic accommodation, they frequently offer a limited menu of high-quality food at very reasonable prices. *Fondas* can be identified by a blue plaque, with a white F painted on the wall.

Merenderos, found all the way along the coast of Spain, are beach restaurants specialising mainly in fish dishes but usually offering omelettes and salads as well. Don't forget to look out for *tapas* bars (*tascas*). There are often two scales of prices in these bars: *a la barra* or *a la mesa* — at the bar or at the table. You pay extra if you sit down, and sometimes even more if you sit outside. But they are still very cheap.

The Spanish eat both dinner and lunch much later than we do, but most restaurants will serve meals from 1pm to 3.30pm and from 8pm till midnight. Prices include taxes and sometimes a service charge. It is still considered appropriate to leave a tip (*una propina*) Ten to twelve per cent should be about right.

BARS AND CAFÉS

Bars generally only serve drinks, while cafés serve both drinks and food — usually snacks. There is no obvious official grading system employed here, but you get the picture from looking at the decor and general presentation. In the fancier places you will be paying for the atmosphere, and perhaps more attentive and obsequious service, rather than better drinks; though here you can often buy cocktails, and good ones, at a fraction of our price. Whichever you choose, the price of a cup of coffee or a glass of wine will buy you a seat for as long as you wish, and, except in very busy resorts in high season, nobody will mind if you sit and nurse one drink all afternoon or evening. Again, prices include service, but it is customary to leave a small tip — 5-10 per cent.

Breakfast is a good meal to eat out — coffee always tastes so much better in a bar. Order doughnuts, sweet cakes or toasted buns — with butter and jam or a little olive oil and garlic. Along with other delights to smear on your toasted bun, you may come across a tub of orange stuff. It is probably 'pig-fat butter' — very much an acquired taste. But you can do nothing better for breakfast than visit a *churrería*. *Churros* are long, thin coils of batter fried in deep, hot oil. They are greasy, delicious and cheap. Dip them in sugar, or in your coffee, tea or chocolate — this makes a most agreeable sludge at the bottom of your cup, which can be eaten with a spoon. *Churros* are everywhere, out on the streets, in barrows, or in tiny corner booths; order about 200 grams per person and eat them straight from the paper.

More refined in the cake line are the *pastelerías* (bakers' shops). The quality and variety of Spanish cakes is really formidable. You enter a *pastelería* at your peril, for so delicious and alluring are the wares that even those with the strongest willpower will succumb. Many serve tea and coffee as well as ice-creams, in which case they may be called *heladerías*.

EATING OUT

Vocabulary

Aperitif	*Aperitivo*
Bacon	*Tocino*
Bread	*Pan*
Breakfast	*Desayuno*
Butter	*Mantequilla*
Cereal	*Cereale*
Cheese	*Queso*
Chips	*Patas Fritas*
Chocolate	*Chocolate*
Coffee	*Café*
Dessert	*Postre*
Dinner	*La cena*
Eggs	*Huevos*
— boiled	— *huevo cocido*
— fried	— *huevo fritos*
— scrambled	— *huevo revueltos*
Fruit	*Frutas*
Fish	*Pescado*
Hot	*Caliente*

Ice-cream	*Helado*
Jam	*Mermelada/confitura*
Lunch	*El almuerzo*
Marmalade	*Mermelada con Naranja*
Meat	*Carne*
Medium	*Regulár*
Milk	*Leche*
Mustard	*Mostaza*
Oil	*Aceite*
Pepper	*Pimienta*
Poultry	*Aves*
Rice	*Arróz*
Roast	*Al horno*
Rare	*Medio crudo*
Salad	*Ensalada*
Salt	*Sal*
Sauce	*Salsa*
Soup	*Sopa*
Sautéed	*Salteado*
Stewed	*Estofado*
Tea	*Té*
Toast	*Tostada*
Vegetables	*Legumbres*
Vinegar	*Vinagre*
Well-done	*Muy hecho*

Phrases

Could we have a table?	*Nos puede dar una mesa?*
The menu, please	*La carta por favor*
Do you have …?	*Tienen …?*
I'd like some …	*Quisiera …*
What do you recommend?	*Qué me aconseja?*
Can you recommend a local speciality?	*Puede aconsejarnos un especialidad local?*
Nothing more, thank you	*Nada mas, gracias*
I'd like to pay	*Quisiera pagar*
The bill please	*La cuenta por favor*

RECIPES

These recipes all serve four people unless otherwise stated. All weights and measures are given in the local metric amounts in which you will be buying the ingredients. A table of weights and measures is given at the end of the book for reference.

SOUPS, SALADS, STARTERS AND EGG DISHES

Soups

Caldo Haba (Bean, Ham and Sausage Soup)
Gazpacho
Sopa de Ajo (Garlic Soup)
Sopa de Almendras (Almond Soup)
Sopa a la Marinera (Fisherman's Soup)
Sopa de Tomates y Mariscos (Tomato and Shellfish Soup)
Sopa de Escaldada (Vegetable Soup)

Salads

Ensalada de Arróz (Rice Salad)
Ensalada de Espárragos (Asparagus Salad)
Ensalada Isabella (Celery, Apple and Potato Salad)
Ensalada de Judías Verdes (Green Bean Salad)
Ensalada San Isidro (Tuna and Egg Salad)
Ensalada de Tomates 1 (Tomato Salad 1)
Ensalada de Tomates 2 (Tomato Salad 2)
Xato (Endive Salad in Piquant Sauce)

Starters

Champiñones con Jamón (Mushrooms with Ham)
Gambas al Ajillo (Prawns in Garlic)
Tomates Rellenos (Stuffed Tomatoes)
Tomates al Horno (Basil Baked Tomatoes)

Egg Dishes

Huevos a la Flamenca (Eggs Flamenca)
Huevos con Chorizo (Scrambled Eggs with Sausage)
Tortilla Español 1 (Spanish Omelette 1)
Tortilla Español 2 (Spanish Omelette 2)

Caldo Haba (Bean, Ham and Sausage Soup)

This soup is a meal in itself and should be eaten with lots of crusty Spanish bread. It is quite time-consuming to prepare, but it is well worth the effort.

2.5 litres water	1 teaspoon salt
180g white beans	Freshly ground black pepper
250g 'Serrano' ham (or similar cured ham) chopped into small cubes	150g smoked, garlic sausage
	2 medium potatoes, peeled and chopped
1 medium onion, finely chopped	

Bring the water to the boil over a high heat. Add the beans and boil for two minutes. Remove the pan from the heat and set aside, leaving the beans to soak for 1½ hours. Replace the pan on the heat and add the ham, onion, salt and pepper. Bring to the boil and remove any scum from the surface with a metal spoon. Reduce the heat and simmer for 1½ hours. Puncture the sausage with a fork and add to the pan with the potatoes. Cook for a further 30 minutes or until the beans and potatoes are tender. Remove the sausage, skin it, slice it and put the slices back into the soup. Add more salt and pepper if required.

Gazpacho

There are many different versions of this delicious cold soup. Every region has its own way of preparing Gazpacho and it really isn't necessary to be too precise about measuring the ingredients. Use the following recipe as a general guideline, but you can leave out the pepper and/or the cucumber if you wish.

250g ripe tomatoes	1 small Spanish onion
60g white bread	Half a small cucumber
4 tablespoons olive oil	1 tablespoon wine vinegar
½ litre water	
1 small green pepper	

Garnish (Optional)

Finely diced onion, green or red pepper, cucumber   *Fried croutons*

Peel the tomatoes. Roughly chop the tomatoes, pepper, cucumber and onion and put in a blender with the oil, garlic, bread and some of the water. Blend until smooth. Add the remaining water, vinegar and season to taste. Add the garnish to the soup or serve in separate bowls. This soup is best eaten well chilled.

Sopa de Ajo (Garlic Soup)

This soup does, of course, taste of garlic, but not as strongly as you might imagine. Boiling garlic reduces its strong flavour and the result is subtle and delicious.

16 cloves garlic
Bay leaf
1 teaspoon dried thyme
2 teaspoons dried sage
1 teaspoon salt
2 cloves

1 litre water
3 egg-yolks
4 tablespoons olive oil
2 tablespoons chopped parsley

Put garlic, bay leaf, thyme, sage, salt and cloves in a large saucepan. Add the water and bring to the boil. Reduce the heat and simmer for 30 minutes. Strain the soup, but press the remaining juice from the garlic cloves through the strainer. Set aside. Put egg yolks in a large bowl and whisk until thick and creamy. Add the oil, a drop at a time, beating continuously until the oil is incorporated and the mixture is smooth. Reheat the soup and slowly beat into the egg and oil mixture. Sprinkle with parsley and serve immediately.

Sopa de Almendras (Almond Soup)

100g blanched almonds
2 cloves garlic
2 tablespoons olive oil

2 teaspoons wine vinegar
250ml water

Put almonds, garlic, olive oil and salt in blender or crush well with a fork. Slowly mix in the water. Chill the soup. Add the vinegar just before serving. Sprinkle with chopped parsley if desired.

Sopa a la Marinera (Fisherman's Soup)

1 kg white fish (i.e. Pagro or
   Dorada)
2 large Spanish onions
2 hard-boiled eggs, sliced
3 slices white bread, broken
   into small pieces

8 tablespoons olive oil
Large sprig parsley
1 litre water
2 cloves garlic
Salt and pepper to taste

Clean the fish and place in a large saucepan covered with the water. Place over a medium heat. Bring to boil and simmer for 5 minutes. Remove the fish and bone. Reserve the cooking water. Chop the onions, garlic and parsley and sauté gently in the oil. When the onion begins to turn golden, transfer the mixture to a large saucepan and add the boned fish. Add the cooking liquid to the vegetables, together with the bread and seasoning. Cover and simmer for 20 minutes. Garnish with sliced egg. Serve immediately.

Sopa de Tomates y Mariscos
(Tomato and Shellfish Soup)

3 large onions, sliced
1 kg tomatoes, peeled and
   chopped
1 clove garlic, crushed
200 g (approx) cooked
   prawns, mussels and
   clams

2 tablespoons olive oil
600 ml fish stock
20 g small pasta noodles
salt and pepper
Tablespoon parsley, finely
   chopped

Heat olive oil in a large frying pan and cook the onions until soft, but not brown. Add chopped tomatoes, garlic, salt and pepper. Simmer for 5 minutes. Add fish stock and simmer for further 20 minutes. Strain soup or purée in blender. Return to the pan and add the pasta noodles and shellfish. Simmer gently until the pasta is tender. Sprinkle with parsley and serve.

Sopa de Escaldada (Vegetable Soup)

250 g brown lentils
1 kg artichokes, broad beans,
   spinach, cabbage, peas
   (any combination may be
   used)

100 g bacon
Salt and pepper to taste
Water

Clean the lentils carefully. Be sure to remove any grit. Boil in salted water until tender. Chop the vegetables into small pieces and boil in a saucepan with the bacon and just enough cold water to cover all the ingredients. When the lentils are ready, purée in a blender or mash through a sieve. Add to the vegetables and bacon. Continue to simmer over a low heat, adding more water, if necessary, until a thick consistency is obtained. Place a slice of bread, crust removed, in each soup bowl and pour the soup over the top. Serve immediately.

Ensalada de Arróz (Rice Salad)

100g long-grain rice
8 small tomatoes
1 medium green pepper

Vinaigrette dressing (see p. 120)

Cook rice and drain well. Blanch and peel the tomatoes and chop. De-seed the pepper and cut into thin strips. Toss the tomatoes and peppers in the vinaigrette and mix into the cold, cooked rice.

Ensalada de Espárragos (Asparagus Salad)

500g green asparagus
1 tablespoon wine vinegar
3 tablespoons olive oil

1 garlic clove, crushed
Half teaspoon paprika
Salt and pepper

Cook the asparagus following the basic preparation instructions on page 28 (if you wish, you can substitute tinned asparagus). In a bowl mix the oil, vinegar, garlic, paprika, salt and pepper and toss the asparagus in the dressing. Leave to marinade for one hour before serving.

Ensalada Isabella (Celery, Apple and Potato Salad)

2 celery hearts
½kg cooked potatoes
4 apples
1 clove garlic, finely
*   chopped*

1 egg-yolk
Pepper and salt
Oil
Lemon juice

Slice the potatoes and chop the celery. Peel and slice the apples. Crush the chopped garlic in a bowl with a fork and add the egg-yolk and seasoning. Stir in the oil, a drop at a time, until the mixture thickens. Add lemon juice to taste.

Toss apples, potatoes and celery in the garlic mayonnaise and serve.

Ensalada de Judías Verdes (Green Bean Salad)

500g green beans
Vinaigrette dressing (see p. 120)

Crushed garlic clove

Trim the beans and cook until just tender. Drain well and toss in vinaigrette to which a little crushed garlic has been added. Serve cold.

Ensalada San Isidro (Tuna and Egg Salad)

1 medium lettuce
1 small tin tuna
1 small onion, finely
  chopped
2 hard-boiled eggs

4 tablespoons oil
50g green olives
1 tablespoon vinegar
Salt and pepper to taste

Wash and chop the lettuce and place in a salad bowl. Add the tuna fish, cut into small chunks, together with the onion and olives. Cut the eggs into quarters and place on top of the salad. Beat the oil, vinegar and salt together until well blended and pour over the salad. Toss and serve.

Ensalada de Tomates 1 (Tomato Salad 1)

Tiny, sweet tomatoes are widely available throughout Spain but they are especially good in the Canary Islands. This simple salad is quick and easy to prepare.

20 small, firm tomatoes
2 medium or one large
  Spanish onion
Salt to taste

Sugar to taste
Vinaigrette dressing (see p. 120)

Wash the tomatoes and slice in half with a sharp knife. Sprinkle with sugar (about one teaspoonful) and set aside. Slice the onions very thinly and mix with the tomatoes. Dress with a light vinaigrette dressing and serve.

Ensalada de Tomates 2 (Tomato Salad 2)

This salad is also very simple but uses the larger 'beefsteak' tomatoes. Choose firm, unblemished tomatoes and don't worry if they are tinged with green — the flavour will still be excellent.

4 large tomatoes
1 large Spanish onion
Salt to taste

Vinaigrette dressing (see p. 120)

Slice the tomatoes and the onions as thinly as possible. Sprinkle lightly with salt and dress with an olive oil-based vinaigrette dressing.

Xato (Endive Salad in Piquant Sauce)

1 large head of endive
50g almonds
4 cloves garlic, peeled
Half a small, fresh chilli
   pepper

6 tablespoons olive oil
2 tablespoons wine vinegar
Salt to taste

Wash the endive and chop roughly. Place in a salad bowl and set aside. Crush the almonds, garlic and chilli in a blender or with a fork. Add the oil slowly until the mixture thickens. Add vinegar and salt. Mix well and pour over the chopped endives. Toss well. Serve as an accompaniment to *chorizo* sausage or ham.

Champiñones con Jamón (Mushrooms with Ham)

½kg mushrooms
200g York ham, cubed
2 tablespoons olive oil
1 tablespoon fresh
   breadcrumbs

1 tablespoon chopped
   parsley
2 cloves garlic, crushed
100ml sherry
Black pepper

In a heavy frying pan heat the oil and sauté the ham. Peel the mushrooms and add to the ham. Sauté for 10 minutes. Turn the heat up and add the breadcrumbs, parsley and garlic. Stir well. Add the sherry and the black pepper. Simmer for 10 minutes. Serve hot with crusty bread.

Gambas al Ajillo (Prawns in Garlic)

½kg small prawns in their
　shells
4 tablespoons olive oil
30g butter
4 cloves garlic, peeled and
　sliced very thinly
1 tablespoon lemon juice
1 tablespoon dry sherry

Half teaspoon paprika
1 small red chilli pepper,
　seeds removed and finely
　chopped
Half tablespoon chopped
　parsley
Ground black pepper

Heat the oil and butter in a heavy frying pan. Add the prawns and the garlic and sauté over a high heat for about 3 minutes. Add the lemon juice, sherry, paprika, chilli, salt and pepper. Sprinkle with parsley and serve while still very hot.

Tomates Rellenos (Stuffed Tomatoes)

4 medium-size ripe but firm
　tomatoes
100g fresh breadcrumbs
1 medium onion, finely
　chopped
Clove garlic, crushed
10 black or green olives,
　chopped

8 anchovy fillets, chopped
4 tablespoons olive oil
1 tablespoon parsley, finely
　chopped
Salt and pepper to taste
Teaspoon mixed herbs
30g butter

Cut the tops off the tomatoes and scoop out the flesh. Be careful not to pierce the skins. Heat the oil in a frying pan and add the chopped onion and crushed garlic. Sauté gently for 5 minutes. Add the breadcrumbs, parsley, anchovies, olives, salt and pepper and herbs. Stir well and remove from the heat. With a teaspoon pile the mixture into the prepared tomato shells. Top each tomato with a knob of butter and bake in a moderate oven for 20 minutes. Serve hot or cold.

Tomates al Horno (Basil Baked Tomatoes)

100g butter
2 large onions, thinly sliced
　and pushed out into rings
10 medium-size tomatoes,
　thinly sliced
2 tablespoons chopped fresh
　basil or 2 teaspoons of
　dried basil

6 grindings black pepper
1 teaspoon salt
1 teaspoon sugar
90g fresh white
　breadcrumbs

Preheat the oven to fairly hot (200°C/400°F) and lightly grease an oven-proof dish with one tablespoon of the butter. Melt two tablespoons of the butter in a large frying pan over a low heat. Put in the onion rings and fry for 10 minutes or until tender but not brown. Remove the pan from the heat. Put a layer of onion rings in the bottom of the oven-proof dish, sprinkle with a little basil and cover with a layer of tomato slices. Add a little pepper and salt and a sprinkling of sugar. Dot with some of the remaining butter cut into small pieces. Repeat the layers until all ingredients have been used. Finish with a layer of breadcrumbs and dot with remaining butter. Bake for 30 minutes. Serve hot.

Huevos a la Flamenca (Eggs Flamenca)

3 tablespoons olive oil
1 large onion, thinly sliced
1 garlic clove, finely chopped
4 medium-size ripe tomatoes, chopped
6 eggs

8 thick slices chorizo *sausage*
1 small green pepper, cored, seeded and thinly sliced
1 teaspoon salt
1 teaspoon black pepper

In a large frying pan, heat the oil over a moderate heat. Add the onion and garlic and fry, stirring occasionally for 5 minutes. Add the tomatoes, sausage slices, green pepper, salt and pepper. Reduce heat to low and simmer for 10 minutes, stirring occasionally. Remove the pan from the heat and turn the mixture into a shallow oven-proof dish. Break the eggs on top and place the dish in a preheated oven (200°C/ 400°F) for approximately 15 minutes or until the eggs are set. Serve immediately.

Huevos con Chorizo (Scrambled Eggs with Sausage)

2 medium-size green peppers, seeded and thinly sliced
2 tablespoons olive oil
½kg chorizo *sausage cut into thin slices*
1 garlic clove, crushed

4 ripe tomatoes, peeled and roughly chopped
4 tablespoons water
6 eggs, lightly beaten
Salt
Black pepper

Pour the oil into a heavy frying pan and place over a high heat. When hot, add the sausage slices and fry, turning frequently until brown. Stir in the garlic and tomatoes, water and seasoning. Cook gently, stirring occasionally until the mixture thickens. Add peppers and cook for another 5 minutes. Pour the beaten eggs into the frying pan and cook over a low heat until the eggs are just set. Serve immediately.

Tortilla Español (Spanish Omelette)

Here are two recipes for Spanish omelette. The first is the simple, traditional omelette and is not as bland as you might expect from the simple ingredients used. It is excellent with a simple salad and bread.

Method 1

2 large potatoes	Salt
2 medium Spanish onions	3 tablespoons olive oil
4 eggs	

Dice the potatoes and the onions finely. Heat 3 tablespoons of olive oil in a frying pan and add the vegetables and seasoning. Cover the pan to retain the moisture. Simmer, stirring occasionally, until tender. Meanwhile, separate the eggs and beat the whites until light and airy. Beat the yolks into the whites. Remove the vegetables from the pan and add to the egg mixture. Reheat the oil remaining in the pan and, just as it begins to smoke, pour in the egg and vegetable mixture. Lower the heat and cook for 3 minutes. Cover the pan with a large plate and turn upside down. Slide the inverted omelette back into the frying pan and cook briefly on the other side. Alternatively, grill to brown it on top.

Method 2

3 tablespoons olive oil	1 medium potato, diced
1 large onion, chopped	1 carrot, diced
1 small red pepper, cored, seeded and chopped	2 cloves garlic, crushed
1 small green pepper, cored, seeded and chopped	Salt and pepper
	4 eggs

Heat the oil in a frying pan and add the chopped vegetables and garlic. Cover and simmer for 10 minutes, stirring occasionally. Season well. Separate the eggs. Beat the whites until light and airy and then beat in the egg-yolks. Turn up the heat and add the egg mixture to the vegetables. Cook until set and finish under a pre-heated grill if you prefer a 'drier' omelette.

MAIN COURSES

Paella
Riñones al Jerez (Kidneys in Sherry)
Pollo con Arróz (Chicken with Rice)
Cordero Español (Spanish Lamb)
Conejo al Ajillo y Tomate (Rabbit with Garlic and Tomatoes)
Pollo al Ajillo con Almendras (Chicken with Garlic and Almonds)
Pollo al Jerez (Roast Chicken with Sherry)
Mero al Jerez (Grouper cooked in Sherry)
Merluza a la Marinera (Hake with Almonds, Tomatoes and Parsley)
Filete de Pescado al Mediterraneo (Fillets of Fish Mediterranean Style)
Pez Espada con Almendras (Swordfish with Almonds)
Almejas a la Marinera (Clams with Tomato and Garlic)
Estofado del Mar (Mediterranean Fish Stew)
Filetes de Ternera Empanados (Breaded Veal Cutlets)
Arróz con Carne de Cerdo (Rice with Pork)
Zarzuela (Seafood 'Medley')
Chuletas de Cordero a la Navarra (Lamb Chops à la Navarra)

Paella

There are many versions of this classic Spanish recipe. Some use very simple, basic ingredients while the more extravagant versions are made with expensive shellfish, such as lobster. The following recipe can be used as a guideline. Prepare your own version with whatever you have at hand.

1 kg chicken, cut into small joints
1 large Spanish onion
1 carrot
1 celery stalk
1 bay leaf
Pepper
Salt
350g unshelled prawns
10 mussels or small clams (or a mixture of both)
6 tablespoons olive oil
2 cloves garlic, crushed
100g peas
3 ripe tomatoes, peeled and chopped
1 small green pepper, deseeded and chopped
450g rice
Teaspoon ground saffron, or one filament, soaked in a little warm water for 30 minutes
½ tablespoon of parsley
1 small red pepper, seeded and thinly sliced
8 giant prawns, unshelled

111

In a large, deep heavy pan, heat the olive oil over a moderate heat. Add the chicken pieces and fry, turning occasionally for 10-15 minutes, or until the chicken is brown on all sides. Remove the chicken pieces and keep hot. Add the onion, carrot, celery and garlic and stir-fry gently for 5-7 minutes. Add the tomatoes, green pepper, salt and pepper and cook for 10 minutes, stirring occasionally. Add the rice to the pan and fry, stirring continuously, for 3 minutes. Add the stock or water and the saffron water to the pan and bring to the boil. Reduce the heat to low and stir in the peas. Return the chicken pieces to the pan and cook gently for 15 minutes. Add the smaller prawns, mussels and/or clams and cook for a further 5 minutes or until the liquid is absorbed. Remove from the heat. Sprinkle with parsley and garnish with red pepper slices and giant prawns. Serve immediately.

Riñones al Jerez (Kidneys in Sherry)

½kg beef kidney	Pepper
1 tablespoon olive oil	Parsley
4 tablespoons dry sherry	4 slices of white bread cut
2 tablespoons tomato purée	into triangles
Salt	

Cut the kidneys into thin slices and season well. Heat the oil in a frying pan and sauté the kidneys for 5 minutes. Heat the sherry in a heavy saucepan until it has reduced to half the quantity. Add the tomato paste and salt and pepper. Pour over the kidneys and cook for 10 minutes. Fry the triangles of bread until crisp and golden. Place on top of the kidney mixture, sprinkle with parsley and serve.

Pollo con Arróz (Chicken with Rice)

1 chicken, jointed	3 medium tomatoes
½kg lean pork, roughly chopped	2 red peppers
6 tablespoons olive oil	800ml stock
2 cloves garlic	Pinch saffron
1kg rice	150ml sherry

Heat the olive oil in a frying pan and fry the chicken and the pork until lightly browned. Remove and place in a casserole. Chop the onion and garlic and fry them in the remaining oil until golden brown. Add the rice and cook for 2 minutes, then add the sliced tomatoes and red peppers and cook for another 2 minutes. Pour this mixture over the top of the chicken. Bring the stock to the boil and add to the chicken with the saffron and the sherry. Simmer over a gentle heat for about one hour or until the chicken is tender and the rice soft.

Cordero Español (Spanish Lamb)

1 medium-size leg or
  shoulder of lamb (2$\frac{1}{2}$kg
  approx)
50g butter
1 clove garlic
1 bay leaf

Salt
Pepper
200ml white wine
1 tablespoon chopped
  parsley

Place the meat in a casserole with the butter, chopped garlic, bay leaf, salt and pepper. Cook in a moderate oven, basting occasionally until the meat is brown. Add the wine and continue cooking until the meat is tender, basting frequently. Remove the meat and keep hot. Strain the gravy, add the parsley and seasoning if necessary. Return the meat to the casserole and pour the gravy over the top. Serve.

Conejo al Ajillo y Tomate (Rabbit with Garlic and Tomatoes)

1 medium-sized rabbit,
  jointed
1 large onion, chopped
2 cloves garlic, crushed
1 garlic clove cut in half
1 green pepper, chopped
3 large tomatoes, skinned
  and chopped

200ml white wine
3 tablespoons olive oil
Salt
Pepper
Sprig parsley
Pinch thyme
Bay leaf

Rub the cut clove of garlic over the rabbit pieces. Mix the crushed garlic with the wine in a medium-size bowl and put the rabbit pieces in the mixture to marinade for one hour. Remove the rabbit pieces. Strain the marinade and reserve the liquid. Heat the oil in a casserole and brown the rabbit pieces on all sides. Remove the rabbit pieces and sauté the onion and green pepper until soft. Return the rabbit pieces to the pan and add the tomatoes, herbs, reserved marinade and garlic. Stir and simmer for 2 hours. Rice and salad are the best accompaniment to this dish.

Pollo al Ajillo con Almendras (Chicken with Garlic and Almonds)

8 chicken pieces
4 tablespoons olive oil
1 large Spanish onion, finely
   chopped
2 garlic cloves, crushed
1 medium green pepper,
   chopped
Salt
Cayenne pepper

Parsley sprig
Pinch thyme
Bay leaf
Seasoned flour
200ml white wine
200ml chicken stock
100g ground almonds
2 yolks of hard-boiled eggs

Shake the chicken pieces in a paper bag with seasoned flour until evenly coated. Heat the oil over a moderate heat in a large, flame-proof casserole. Add the onion, garlic and green pepper and cook for 5 minutes or until they are soft. Remove from the casserole, turn the heat to high and add the chicken pieces. Fry until well browned all over. Return the vegetables to the casserole, together with the wine, stock, seasoning and herbs. Bring to the boil, cover and simmer for about 45 minutes or until the chicken is tender.

In a mixing-bowl mash the hard egg-yolks with a little of the cooking juices. When it is smooth and creamy add the ground almonds. Add this mixture slowly to the casserole, stirring continuously. Cook for a further 5 minutes, then remove the chicken with a slotted spoon. Bring the sauce to the boil and keep boiling until the liquid has reduced to approximately half and the sauce has a good, creamy consistency. Pour over the chicken and serve.

Pollo al Jerez (Roast Chicken with Sherry)

8 chicken pieces
3 tablespoons olive oil
1 sprig parsley, chopped
2 tablespoons lard
100ml sherry

2 cloves garlic, roughly
   chopped
Salt
Pepper

Pour the oil into a roasting pan, add the chicken pieces and sprinkle with salt, pepper and parsley. Add the sherry and the chopped garlic. Smear the chicken with lard and place in the oven at 180°C (350°F) for about 50 minutes, basting every 10 minutes. If the sauce evaporates too fast, add a little water. Serve with fried potatoes and a vegetable.

Mero al Jerez (Grouper Cooked in Sherry)

1 kg grouper, halibut or
   similar, cut into steaks
100 g flaked almonds
2 cloves garlic, crushed
100 ml sherry

3 tablespoons olive oil
Salt
Pepper
2 sprigs parsley, chopped

Place the fish in an oven-proof casserole dish. Pour over the oil, almonds, garlic and sherry. Sprinkle with salt and pepper. Bake for 30 minutes with the oven at 180°C (Gas mark 4), basting frequently. Sprinkle with the parsley, cook for a further 3 minutes and serve.

Merluza a la Marinera (Hake with Almonds, Tomatoes and Parsley)

1 kg filleted hake
3 tablespoons olive oil
1 finely chopped onion
2 crushed garlic cloves
Salt
Pepper
Mixed herbs
100 g ground almonds

50 g breadcrumbs
½ kg tomatoes, peeled and
   chopped
¾ litre hot water
50 g flaked almonds
2 large sprigs chopped
   parsley

Heat the oil over a moderate heat in a large frying pan. Fry the onion and garlic. As the onion turns golden, add half the parsley, the almonds, breadcrumbs and tomatoes. Cook for a further 5 minutes, then set aside. Place the fish in a large baking dish, pour on the hot water, lemon juice, salt, pepper and herbs. Cover the dish and place in a hot oven for 10 minutes or until the fish is soft and flaky. Transfer the fillets to a warmed serving dish. Add half a cup of the cooking liquid from the fish to the sauce, return to the heat and stir until smooth. Pour over the fish and sprinkle with the rest of the parsley and the flaked almonds.

Filete de Pescado al Mediterraneo (Fillets of Fish Mediterranean Style)

1 kg white fish fillets
1 large onion, finely
   chopped
4 tomatoes, peeled and
   chopped

1 sprig chopped parsley
100 g shelled prawns
2 tablespoons olive oil
1 cup white wine
2 egg-yolks

200g mushrooms
Salt
Pepper

½ cup cream
Juice of 1 lemon

Fry the onion in the oil over a moderate heat in a large frying pan. When the onion starts to turn golden, add the mushrooms, tomatoes, salt and pepper. Cook for a further 3 minutes. Add the fish fillets and wine. Bring to the boil, cover the pan and simmer for 10 minutes. When the fish is soft and flaky, transfer to a heated serving dish. Boil the remaining liquid in the pan and reduce by half. Meanwhile, beat the egg-yolks with the cream and add two tablespoons of the cooking liquid to the egg mixture together with the lemon juice. Add the egg mixture to the liquid remaining in the pan and stir for 3-4 minutes over a moderate heat, taking care not to let the mixture boil. As it thickens, add the prawns and cook for 2-3 minutes. Pour over the warm fish fillets, sprinkled with the parsley and serve with new potatoes and salad.

Pez Espada con Almendras (Swordfish with Almonds)

4 large swordfish steaks
4 tablespoons olive oil
Salt

Cayenne pepper
100g flaked almonds
Juice of 2 lemons

Rub salt and Cayenne pepper into the fish steaks. Heat the oil over a moderate heat and fry the almonds for 4 minutes. Remove the almonds. Raise the heat to moderately high and fry the fish steaks on both sides until they are just turning brown. Add the lemon juice and almonds. When the mixture comes to the boil, lower the heat, cover the pan and simmer for about 10 minutes, or until the fish steaks are tender. Good with fried potatoes and a mixed salad.

Almejas a la Marinera (Clams with Tomato and Garlic)

300g small clams or similar
shellfish, in their shells
5 large tomatoes, peeled
and chopped

1 large onion, chopped
2 crushed cloves garlic
½ litre white wine
2 hard-boiled eggs

4 tablespoons olive oil
Salt
Pepper

2 sprigs finely chopped
    parsley
100g breadcrumbs

Separate the whites from the yolks and mash the yolks. Heat the oil in a frying pan. Add the onion and garlic and sauté over a low heat for 5 minutes. Add the tomatoes, bread-crumbs, egg-yolks, salt, pepper and a pinch of parsley. Mash with a wooden spoon over a low heat until the mixture becomes a thick purée. Set aside and keep warm. Place clams in a saucepan, pour on the wine and bring to the boil. Simmer for 10 minutes. Throw away any which have not opened or which float to the surface. Pour the cooking liquid into the tomato purée, stir and season and pour over the clams. Sprinkle with finely chopped egg-whites and parsley and serve with rice and a green salad.

Estofado del Mar (Mediterranean Fish Stew)

1kg fresh white fish
6 medium potatoes, sliced
1 onion, finely chopped
1 chopped celery stalk
5 tablespoons olive oil
2 cloves garlic, one crushed,
    one whole

Salt
Pepper
Bay leaf
1 chopped sprig parsley
1 teaspoon grated orange
    rind
1 cup garlic mayonnaise

Cut the fish into portion-sized pieces and place in a large saucepan. Add the potatoes, chopped onion, celery and crushed garlic. Sprinkle with salt, pepper, parsley and orange rind. Pour on olive oil and enough boiling water to cover. Boil for 15 minutes or until the potatoes are tender. Strain off the liquid into another saucepan and add the garlic mayonnaise. Place the pan over a low heat and simmer for 3 minutes, stirring constantly. Return the thickened sauce to the fish mixture and serve immediately.

Filetes de Ternera Empanados (Breaded Veal Cutlets)

1kg veal chops, thinly cut
3 tablespoons olive oil
1 egg
1 teaspoon lemon juice

Breadcrumbs
Tablespoon chopped parsley
Salt
Pepper

Season the veal chops on both sides. Beat the egg and

lemon juice together. Mix the parsley with the breadcrumbs. Dip the cutlets first into the egg and then into the breadcrumbs, pressing well to ensure the crumbs stick. Heat the oil in a frying pan and fry until the cutlets are golden over a moderate heat.

Arróz con Carne de Cerdo (Rice with Pork)

½kg lean pork, chopped
6 tablespoons olive oil
6 cloves garlic
½kg tomatoes, peeled and
   chopped
4 red peppers, seeded and
   sliced

1 tablespoon chopped
   parsley
Pinch saffron
400g long-grain rice
1 litre boiling water
Salt
Pepper

Heat oil in a flame-proof casserole. Fry the pork until brown on all sides. Remove and set aside. Peel the garlic cloves and sauté in the oil. Set aside. Put the tomatoes and peppers in the frying pan and cook gently until soft. Meanwhile crush the garlic, together with the parsley and saffron, and add to the vegetables together with the pork. Add a little cold water, stir well and cook gently for 5 minutes. Stir in the rice and add the boiling water. Season well. Cover and cook in a preheated oven at 180°C (Gas mark 4) for 30 minutes or until the pork is cooked and the rice tender.

Zarzuela (Seafood 'Medley')

4 tablespoons olive oil
1 onion, finely chopped
6 medium tomatoes, skinned
   and chopped
1 strand saffron soaked in a
   little warm water
50g blanched almonds,
   chopped
300ml white wine
2 garlic cloves, crushed

1 litre mussels, scrubbed and
   bearded
8 large prawns (uncooked)
2 tablespoons fresh parsley
1 medium lobster (cooked),
   halved and cleaned and
   cut into bite-size pieces
450g sole
200g small, peeled prawns
3 tablespoons brandy

Heat oil in a heavy frying pan and fry the onion for 3 minutes. Add the tomatoes. Cook gently till soft and pulpy. Add the saffron water, chopped almonds and salt and pepper to taste. Stir well and set aside. Put the wine, garlic and parsley into a large saucepan and bring to the boil. Add the mussels and the large prawns and simmer gently for 5 minutes. Discard any mussels which have not opened. Set aside the shellfish and add the cooking liquid to the frying pan with the tomatoes, onions, almonds and saffron. Set over a low heat and simmer for 10 minutes. Prepare the lobster and cut the sole into strips. Add the lobster, sole, mussels, large prawns and small peeled prawns to the frying pan and simmer for 5 minutes. Stir in the brandy and serve.

Chuletas de Cordero a la Navarra (Lamb Chops à la Navarra

8 small lamb chops
3 tablespoons olive oil
1 small clove garlic, finely chopped
1 onion, finely chopped

100g lean ham, diced
6 ripe tomatoes, peeled and roughly chopped
200g chorizo, thinly sliced
Salt and pepper

Fry the chops in the oil on both sides until lightly browned and transfer to an oven-proof dish. Keep warm. Add the onions and the garlic to the frying pan and sauté gently until the onion begins to turn transparent. Add the diced ham and the tomatoes. Season and stir over a low heat until the mixture thickens. Pour the sauce over the cutlets and cover with the sliced *chorizo*. Place in a preheated oven (Gas mark 6/200°C for 10 minutes).

SAUCES

Salsa Picante (Piquant Sauce)
Salsa Vinagretta (Vinaigrette Dressing)
Ali-oli (Garlic Sauce)
Salsa Romescu (Romescu Sauce)

Salsa Picante (Piquant Sauce)

1 tablespoon olive oil
1 medium onion, finely chopped
1 small red pepper
360g tomatoes
Bay leaf
Salt and pepper

Mixed herbs
250ml water
150ml white wine
30g butter
30g white flour
Dash Tabasco

Heat the olive oil and fry the chopped onion and garlic. Slice the pepper and tomatoes and add to the pan with the bay leaf, herbs, seasoning and Tabasco. Add the water and the white wine and simmer gently for 20 minutes. Meanwhile blend together the butter and flour. Blend or sieve the contents of the frying pan and return to the pan with the flour and butter mixture. Continue stirring until the sauce thickens. This sauce is excellent with fried fish.

Salsa Vinagretta (Vinaigrette Dressing)

It is important to use a good-quality olive oil for salad dressing. Spanish dressings use rather more oil than the French version.

6 tablespoons olive oil
1 tablespoon wine vinegar
Pinch salt

Pinch sugar
$1/2$ teaspoon mustard powder
Clove garlic

Pour the oil into a bowl and beat in the vinegar, salt, sugar and mustard. Lightly crush the garlic clove and leave in the dressing for 30 minutes. Remove the garlic and beat the dressing well. If you have made more than you need, it will keep well in a screw-top jar in the fridge. Shake well before use.

Ali-oli (Garlic Sauce)

This sauce is superb with fried fish and tastes good as a dip for crisp, fresh vegetables.

4 garlic cloves, peeled
$1/2$ teaspoon salt
2 tablespoons lemon juice

2 egg-yolks
250 ml olive oil

Crush the garlic. In a small bowl add the salt and lemon juice to the garlic and mix thoroughly. Beat in the egg-yolks, one at a time, until the mixture thickens. Continue to beat, adding the oil drop by drop. When you have added about three quarters of the oil you can add the rest, still beating, in a steady stream. The finished sauce should have the consistency of thick cream.

Salsa Romescu (Romescu Sauce)

There are a number of versions of this famous sauce. This one is quite simple and is milder in flavour than most. It is excellent served with fried fish.

3 large, ripe tomatoes
2 medium cloves garlic,
   peeled
2 teasponns Cayenne
   pepper

100g ground almonds
2 tablespoons olive oil
1 tablespoon white wine
   vinegar
Salt

Halve the tomatoes and grill with the garlic cloves until they begin to char. Skin the tomatoes and crush to a pulp. Crush the garlic and put the tomatoes, garlic, Cayenne pepper and almonds in a bowl. Mix together well. Add the oil drop by drop, beating constantly. Add the vinegar and continue to beat until the sauce is thick and well blended. Leave to stand for one hour before serving.

DESSERTS

Naranjas Canela (Oranges with Cinnamon)
Torrijas (Chocolate Fried Bread)
Crema Catalana (Catalan Custard)
Plátanos Fritados (Banana Fritters)
Ensalada de Frutas Champaña (Champagne Fruit Salad)
Naranjas al Vino Blanco (Oranges in White Wine)

There are very few typically Spanish desserts. In the main you are safer sticking to ice cream, which is generally excellent, or to fresh fruit.

Naranjas Canela (Oranges with Cinnamon)

4 large oranges, peeled and
   with pith removed
1/2 teaspoon ground
   cinnamon

2 teaspoons sugar
2 tablespoons orange-
   flavoured liqueur

Using a serrated knife, slice the oranges very thinly crosswise. It is best to do this over a bowl so that you don't lose any juice. Place the orange slices and juice in a serving dish. Sprinkle with the sugar, cinnamon and liqueur. Place in the fridge and chill for at least 30 minutes before serving.

Torrijas (Chocolate Fried Bread)

4 slices stale bread cut 1/2
   inch thick
1 egg-yolk
300ml milk

1 tablespoon sherry
Olive oil
2 teaspoons sugar
Grated chocolate

Cut the bread into fingers. Beat the egg and add the milk and sherry. Dip the bread fingers into this mixture, drain them and then fry in olive oil until golden brown. Sprinkle with caster sugar, cover with grated chocolate, pile onto a warmed serving dish, sprinkle with chocolate again and serve very hot. Delicious.

Crema Catalana (Catalan Custard)

$^1/_2$ litre milk	4 egg-yolks
Grated rind $^1/_2$ a lemon	6 tablespoons sugar
1 cinnamon stick	$1^1/_2$ tablespoons cornstarch

Place the milk, lemon peel and cinnamon stick in a saucepan and bring to the boil. Simmer for 10 minutes, then discard the peel and cinnamon. Beat the egg-yolks together with three tablespoons of sugar until smooth and creamy. Beat in the cornstarch. Stir in 3 tablespoons of the hot milk and then add the egg mixture to the remainder of the milk in the saucepan. Cook, stirring constantly, over a moderate heat for about 5 minutes or until thick and smooth. Do not boil. Pour the mixture into shallow dessert dishes and cool. When thoroughly chilled, sprinkle with 1 tablespoon of sugar and place under a hot grill until the sugar begins to bubble. Serve immediately.

Plátanos Fritados (Banana Fritters)

6 medium-size, firm bananas	1 tablespoon brown sugar
125 ml brandy	

Batter

120 g flour	1 tablespoon olive oil
1 teaspoon salt	150 ml milk
2 egg-yolks	4 tablespoons vegetable oil
1 egg-white	2 tablespoons sugar

Peel the bananas and cut in half lengthwise. Put in a shallow dish. Mix the brandy with the brown sugar and pour over the bananas. Leave to marinade for 30 minutes. Sift the flour and salt into a mixing bowl. Make a well in the centre of the flour and drop in the egg-yolks and the olive oil. Add the milk, a little at a time, beating continuously. Mix to a smooth batter. Cover and leave to stand for 30 minutes. Beat the egg-white until stiff and fold into the batter mixture. Heat the oil in a medium-sized frying pan over a moderate heat. Dip the banana halves in the batter and fry in the hot oil until golden brown. Drain on kitchen towels, dredge with sugar and serve immediately.

Ensalada de Frutas Champaña (Champagne Fruit Salad)

3 oranges
1 medium-size ripe
  pineapple
2-3 tablespoons lemon juice
4 ripe pears, peeled, cored
  and sliced
4 apples, peeled, cored and
  sliced
4 bananas, peeled and sliced
100g black grapes

100g green grapes
2 bananas, peeled and sliced
4 peaches, peeled, stoned
  and sliced
1 small ripe, honeydew
  melon
2-3 tablespoons cognac
Half bottle champagne
Sugar to taste

Segment the oranges and put in a large bowl. Peel the pineapple and cut into bite-sized pieces. Add lemon juice to the orange slices and put in the slices of pears, apples and bananas. Dust with sugar and sprinkle with the brandy. Chill. Just before serving add the champagne.

Naranjas al Vino Blanco (Oranges in White Wine)

4 oranges
175g black cherries, stoned
175g green grapes

3 tablespoons sugar
50g flaked almonds
300ml dry, white wine

Remove the peel and the pith from the oranges and cut into thin slices. Arrange the grapes, cherries and orange slices in layers in a bowl, sprinkling each layer with a little sugar and a few flaked almonds. Pour the wine over the fruit and chill for at least 2 hours before serving.

DRINKS

Sangría
Ponche Champaña (Champagne Punch)
Buck's Fizz
Champagne Cocktail
Copa Blanca (White Wine Cup)
Té Helado (Iced Tea)

Sangría

This famous Spanish red wine cup is very easy to make and tastes deceptively innocuous. Use the recipe as a guideline only. The proportions of ingredients used vary considerably and after one or two attempts you will find a version that suits you.

1 bottle red wine
1 orange, thinly sliced
1 lime, sliced
1 lemon, sliced
Juice of 1 lemon

Juice of 1 orange
Sugar to taste
500ml soda water
300ml Spanish brandy
Ice cubes

Pour all the ingredients into a large jug. Stir and add ice cubes and indulge yourselves.

Ponche Champaña (Champagne Punch)

Champagne is so cheap in Spain you will find you can afford to push the boat out. Here is a simple Champagne Punch which tastes delicious. If you like your drinks sweet you can add extra sugar as required.

1 lemon, thinly sliced
1 tablespoon sugar
1/2 bottle dry white wine

2 tablespoons lemon juice
1 bottle dry champagne
Ice-cubes

Place the lemon slices in the bottom of a large bowl. Add the sugar and the white wine and stir until the sugar has dissolved. Stir in the lemon juice and add approximately 10 ice-cubes. Put the bowl in the fridge and chill for at least 30 minutes. Just before serving pour over the champagne and serve immediately.

Buck's Fizz

Certainly not Spanish in origin, this is a delicious drink and relatively economical to prepare given the low cost of both oranges and champagne. Do use freshly squeezed orange juice. Canned or carton juice is simply no substitute.

50ml fresh orange juice
Dash grenadine (optional)

100ml dry or medium-dry
champagne, well chilled

Pour the orange juice into a large wine glass and add a dash of grenadine. Top up with the champagne.

Champagne Cocktail

Brandy is an important ingredient in this cocktail and Spanish *coñac* is excellent and quite inexpensive.

30ml (approx) brandy
130ml champagne
  (well chilled)

1 lump sugar
Twist of lemon peel

Place a small sugar lump or half a teaspoon of granulated sugar in a large wine glass. Add the lemon peel and the brandy and top up with champagne.

Copa Blanca (White Wine Cup)

1 bottle dry white wine
1 large lemon, thinly sliced

500ml lemonade
Ice-cubes

Place the ice-cubes and the lemon slices in the bottom of a large jug or bowl. Pour over the white wine. Add the lemonade and serve immediately.

Té Helado (Iced Tea)

This is definitely not a Spanish recipe, but it is an excellent cooling drink for the whole family and is ideal as a thirst-quencher in hot weather.

4 teaspoons tea
500ml boiling water
6 teaspoons sugar

12 ice-cubes
1 sprig mint
1 lemon, sliced

Put the tea in a jug. Pour the boiling water over and stir. Leave to infuse for approximately 3 minutes. Strain the tea and pour back into the jug. Add the sugar and stir well until dissolved. Add the ice-cubes, the mint sprig and the lemon slices. Stir and set aside until tea is well chilled. Add more ice-cubes if necessary.

Weights and Measures

The following tables of solid and liquid measures are approximate.

SOLID

Ounces	Grams
1/2	15
1	30
2	60
2½	75
3	90
3½	100
4	120
5	150
6	180
7	210
8	250
9	280
10	300
11	330
12	360
1 lb	500
2¼	1 kg
3	1½ kg

LIQUID

British Imperial	Metric
1 fl oz	25 ml
2 fl oz	50 ml
3 fl oz	75 ml
4 fl oz	100 ml
5 fl oz	125 ml
½ pt	300 ml
1 pt	600 ml

American	Metric
1 fl oz	30 ml
2 fl oz	60 ml
3 fl oz	90 ml
4 fl oz	120 ml
5 fl oz	150 ml
½ pt	240 ml
1 pt	480 ml

OVEN TEMPERATURES

	Centigrade	Gas	Fahrenheit
Very cool	130°C	½	250°F
	140°C	1	275°F
Cool	150°C	2	300°F
Warm	170°C	3	325°F
Moderate	180°C	4	350°F
Fairly hot	190°C	5	375°F
	200°C	6	400°F
Hot	220°C	7	425°F
Very hot	230°C	8	450°F
	240°C	9	475°F
	250°C	10	500°F

Bibliography

Boxer, Arabella, *Mediterranean Cookbook* (Penguin, Harmondsworth, 1983)

Casas, Penelope, *The Foods and Wines of Spain* (Penguin, Harmondsworth, 1985)

David, Elizabeth, *Mediterranean Food* (Penguin, Harmondsworth, 1955)

Davidson, Alan, *Mediterranean Seafood* (Penguin, Harmondsworth, 1972)

Delegacion Nacional de la Seccion Feminina del Movimiento, *Cocina Regional* (Editorial Almena, Spain, n.d.)

Emery, W.H., *Shopping for Food in Spain* (Lookout Publications, Spain, 1985)

MacMiadhacháin, Anna, *Spanish Regional Cookery* (Penguin, Harmondsworth, 1976)

Index